STERLING SILVER FLATWARE
for Dining Elegance

Richard Osterberg

Photographs by Nancy A. Clark

Clark Art

with
Price
Guide

Schiffer
Publishing Ltd

77 Lower Valley Road, Atglen, PA 19310

Dedication

To my wife, Gail, who proofread my manuscript(s), and
offered encouragement—a special note of grateful appreciation.
I love you!

Printed in China
ISBN: 0-88740-630-0

We are interested in hearing from authors
with book ideas on related topics.

Published by Schiffer Publishing Ltd.
77 Lower Valley Road
Atglen, PA 19310
Please write for a free catalog.
This book may be purchased from the publisher.
Please include $2.95 postage.
Try your bookstore first.

Table of Contents

Acknowledgments

As with any undertaking, family, friends and the encouragement and understanding they offer has much to do with the completion of a project. So it has been with this undertaking. Each of you allowed me to pick and choose from your collections of silver, linen, and crystal in order to put together this text. This book would not have been possible without the special specific help each of you offered. I am deeply indebted to the following people:

Grant and Rosemary Clark, Jane Dickenson, Hilda Ennis, Chuck and Jane Harmon, Bill and Ann Lyles, Michael E. Merrill, Patrick and Shon Miller, Grace Paul, Fred and Susie Osterberg, John and Barbara Peterson, Jim and Jackie Pusey-Standring, David E. Reichard, Martin Sharp, Ann Shirley, Hank Tompson, Marie Whiteside, and Lucille and Bud Zoerb.

Special thanks to Melissa McKee (Gorham) and to Lisa Perry (Reed and Barton) for their letters and assistance. To Robert M. Johnston of the Sterling Silversmiths Guild a specific note of appreciation.

A special note of thanks is given to Michael E. Merrill, who offered encouragement throughout my writing, loaned silver, and introduced me to the Schiffers.

Thanks, thanks, thanks to David E. Reichard of 150 S. Glen Oaks Blvd., Suite 9245, Burbank, California, 91519 for his help with silver and the Haviland China seen throughout the text.

To Calvin E. Wells, who proofread the original manuscript and offered suggestions and comments, my grateful thanks.

Preface

The kinds of serving implements vary from silver manufacturer to silver manufacturer. In the following narrative, examples have been grouped into appropriate categories and as many examples as could be located of each sample have been photographed. The first part is about place pieces, the second about place settings, and the third about serving pieces. In the text when an item is part of a set, like a two-piece salad serving set, the item will be found alphabetically under the item that appears first alphabetically in the set, in this case the salad serving fork. If you are still not able to locate what you want, refer to the Index of Serving Pieces and locate the item you seek. In this index each item of a set will be alphabetized separately. If you still cannot locate the serving item, check under the Index of Place Pieces, since the item you are searching for may actually be an individual place piece.

Throughout the text information about silver, its history and its past, plus great examples of Haviland china will be found (Haviland pieces were kindly contributed by David Reichard). In addition, china examples from Spode, Lenox, Lipper, Coalport, Minton, and Aynsley are shown. Crystal from Stuart, Rogaska, Mikkasa, and New Martensville are used in Part II.

At the end of the book, readers will note a section with charts that can be reproduced for keeping running inventories of their own collections. The purpose of the sheets is to cause readers to ponder and reflect how and when each piece of silver became part of their collections. Readers are advised that for insurance purposes a complete record must be available that has been executed by a silver appraiser. Photographs are also a great help in time of disaster.

Part 1: Place Pieces

Forks, knives, and spoons are so much a part of our everyday lives that it is difficult to realize that they have not always been used. Perhaps spoons evolved as early man used a shell to scoop food, and then added a stick for a handle. The first knives may have been pieces of chipped obsidian or flint that prehistoric people used for cutting meat. Early people probably learned from experience which item cut best. Forks came much, much later.

Spoons were probably the first eating utensil designed from shells. Eventually spoons were carved from wood, then shaped from horn. As early people began to work with various types of metals they eventually turned to fashioning eating implements and then to spoon-shaped utensils. Until early people learned how to combine copper and other metals the items they created did not last long and very few have survived.

Knives have been around a long time, yet few early examples survive because they were continually being used and sharpened which helped wear them out. Knives were made in Sheffield, England, beginning in the early 1200s. The wealthy people of that time used knives made of silver or gold and some even had precious stones set into the handles. People had their own tableware and carried it with them because not everyone had individual implements for the use of their guests. In fact the inns of the day did not furnish guests with knives and spoons.

The shape of knife blades has changed from time to time, for various reasons. It is reported that Cardinal Richelieu made a rule that knives were to be blunt shaped because one of his guests habitually picked his teeth at the table with the point of his knife. This so enraged the cardinal that he ordered that blades of knives used at the dinner table should be blunt (Giblin 1987). Another tale was that it was dangerous to use pointed knives at the table. When tempers flared, blunt knives caused less injury; therefore in 1669 King Louis IV passed a law to make carrying pointed knives illegal.

Another reason for changes in blade shape was style. Today knives come in a large variety of shapes with different styles and sizes in blades. Stainless steel inserts called 'findings' fit into sterling handles and provide the best blades. Before stainless steel, a by-product of World War II, one type of knife blade was plain steel, sometimes silver-plated. The silver reacted to salt and other corrosive materials requiring additional cleaning. The silver-plated blades reacted to many foods and salts and as they wore out, they became pitted or damaged. Many of these knives were thrown out. This accounts for the fact that many old sets have few knives or none at all. Another problem was stress that caused some blades to snap. Now, a number of manufacturers,

usually overseas manufacturers in Asia, Germany, or England produce the blades in all kinds of styles that silversmiths insert into sterling handles.

The fork was the last item to become a part of everyday eating utensils. The first record of one was in an inventory taken in the Italian city of Florence in 1361. By 1533, Catherine de Medici introduced the fork to France. She brought several dozen with her when she arrived in France. The fork was slowly introduced into the homes of the wealthy in France and it was even slower in being introduced into England. In 1611, Thomas Coryate suggested that he was the first Englishman to eat with a fork in London. He had encountered forks during his travels on the Continent. Perhaps the English were reluctant to take to forks because they did not trust anything originating on the Continent, but Giblin reported that by 1650 the fork was in evidence in almost all of England.

Spoons also began to change when forks were introduced. Large spoons became tablespoons, and smaller ones teaspoons. Tea had been introduced into England and the smaller spoons were necessary for stirring sugar and/or cream into the tea. This probably began the differentiation of implements for various foods which continued for many years.

In the next one hundred years, between 1650 and 1750, people changed their style of eating because of the introduction of the fork. With all these changes, the need for books about dining etiquette emerged. One of the first books to appear was written by a French priest who gave explicit instruction as to how to use the knife, fork, and spoon, as well as the table napkin. As the world slipped into the Age of Industrialization, rapid changes took place with the manufacture of silverware. Soon items that had been luxuries became more affordable. Eventually matching sets of silver were manufactured. During the 1840s the process of silver-plating was perfected and basic eating utensils were available for most Americans.

The silver industry developed slowly during the Industrial Revolution. Introduction of machinery made the production of a number of items possible, all of which appeared the same. Previously silver had been handmade and the pieces varied ever so slightly. Shortly after the Civil War, silversmiths began the process of marking items as sterling. The items produced represented a .925% pureness of silver. Some silversmiths marked their sterling silver as '.925' or '925/1000'. The move to sterling grade was a truly significant achievement

At this same time, settlement and exploration of the American west began to expand, and the growth rapidly resulted in finding silver in many mining operations. With the discovery of the vast silver deposits of the Comstock Silver Mine from 1859 to 1862 and again from 1873 to 1882, silver became much more available and eventually more affordable. Other mines were also producing silver. The price of silver had hovered around $1.35 per troy ounce but it suddenly dropped to $.61 per troy ounce because of the volume of silver coming onto the market. The silver industry expanded and the designs of many silver patterns reflected the increased ability of manufacturers to produce pleasing designs and patterns. The increased refinement in everyday dining also added to the expansion of the industry. As silver dropped in price, causing sterling to become more affordable, the manufacturers were busily increasing their production, and the silver designs of the time represented many of the current interests in art and history. Design became important and schools specializing in the study of design began in New England about the time of the end of the Civil War.

Several silver manufacturers in the United States traveled to England about this time and returned with designers and workers. One of the truly outstanding geniuses from England was William C. Codman, one of Gorham's early designers. He produced a number of important designs, some of which survive almost one hundred years after their introduction. He also was very important in the development of Gorham's *Martelé*, or hammered silver. All of the silver manufacturers had creative people at work in design and production. Reed and Barton had Ernest Meyer, who was responsible for *Francis I*, the most popular pattern for that company.

One of the best examples of burgeoning worldwide recognition of silver was the public's response to the display of Tiffany and Company at the Paris Exposition held in 1878. The company received numerous awards for their silver designs and especially for their display of the Mackay silver service, designed by Tiffany's Edward Moore. The Mackay family owned part of the Comstock Mine and their service was made by Tiffany from their own silver deposits. Tiffany required the work of over two hundred men working for two years to complete the service of approximately 1,250 pieces of flatware and hollow-ware. Tiffany was perhaps the most exclusive American silver manufacturer. Its silver was heavier in weight, had distinctive designs, and was exclusive because it had to be purchased at Tiffany's own stores.

This chapter focuses on the items that have been produced in the United States as individual place pieces. Forks will be discussed first, followed by spoons, knives and then a category called children's silver. Other unusual place pieces will be discussed in the final section.

Forks

Dinner forks were the beginning of the many types of forks that were to be produced by American silver manufacturers. As various foods were introduced into the American diet, specific forks were designed to eat the new foods. Exceptions to this exist, but they are in the specific design of the item. Even though some patterns matched the earlier produced forks, the width of the tines varied. Collectors may notice that the width of tines of forks within a pattern may vary.

Dinner Forks

The largest individual fork is the dinner fork. They were originally called table forks, and eventually evolved into dinner forks. Currently, Wallace Silversmiths has recently begun to call the dinner-size fork in their patterns a 'Place Fork, Large'. This may also result in nomenclature changes by some other manufacturers.

Figure 1.1, Dinner Forks: Reed and Barton's *Marlborough*, 7 3/4"; Towle's *King Richard*, 7 7/8"; Reed and Barton's *Francis I*, 7 27/32"; Gorham's *Sovereign*, 7 13/16"; *Lancaster*, 7 5/8"; Whiting's *Louis XV*, 7 1/2"; Reed and Barton's *Hepplewhite*, 7 3/4"; Gorham's *Strasbourg*, 7 9/16"; and Durgin's *Dauphin*, 7 9/16".

Place Forks

After World War II requests poured in to silver manufacturers for a fork sized between the large dinner fork and the sometimes too small luncheon fork. The result was the place fork. It was mid-sized between the two, not as heavy and large as a dinner fork and easier to balance and hold. For a short time around World War II, some manufacturers even made a grill fork, with short tines and a long handle.

Figure 1.2, Place Forks: Gorham's *Strasbourg*, 7 9/16"; *La Scala*, 7 1/2"; Stieff's *Corsage*, 8 7/8"; Gorham's *Buttercup*, 7 1/2"; and Wallace's *Grand Colonial*, 7 1/4".

Luncheon or Dessert Forks

Luncheon forks were at first called dessert forks. As more silverware was introduced, a separate fork called the dessert fork was made in some patterns. Eventually this fork became best known as the luncheon fork. Much smaller than the large dinner fork, it was much more managable for many people. Women especially found the smaller fork much more utilitarian.

Figure 1.3, Luncheon/Dessert Forks:
Top row: Gorham's *King Edward*, 7 1/8"; Stieff's *Corsage*, 7 1/16"; Gorham's *Strasbourg*, 7"; Towle's *King Richard*, 7 3/8"; Whiting's *Louis XV*, 6 7/8"; Gorham's *Chantilly*, 7"; International's *Royal Danish*, 7 3/32"; Gorham's *Sovereign*, 7 5/8".
Bottom row: Gorham's *Lancaster*, 7"; International's *Prelude*, 7 7/32"; Gorham's *Buttercup*, 7"; Durgin's *Dauphin*, 7"; Dominick and Haff's *Priscilla*, 7 5/32"; Reed and Barton's *Francis I*, 7 1/8"; and *Marlborough*, 7 3/16".

Salad Forks, Large

In some old patterns salad forks were not made, but fish or pie forks may be found that can be used as salad forks. Salad forks were introduced about one hundred years ago. Some patterns had salad forks added later because the pattern sold well and a demand existed for a salad fork. The need was probably coupled with the increased availability of salad-making vegetables due to the new refrigerated train cars that began to appear in the 1880s. Salad forks cannot be identified by counting the tines or by the fact that one of the tines has a cutting edge.

Some salad forks may be found that have gold-washing on the tines. The gold wash acts as a barrier to acidic foods which cause tarnish. Many manufacturers used special processes for gold-washing bowls and tines. Different colors of gold were evident, such as yellow gold, rose gold, and even orange gold. (Another special effect was a textured finish that resembled the skin of an orange.) Gold-washing is especially helpful when the host cannot always take time to wash forks between courses.

Most people do not have servants available to perform the task, but the gold-washing does help retard tarnish. It may also be helpful to place a container filled with hot soapy water in the sink to rinse the forks well and then immerse the forks into the hot soapy water until later, when they can be individually hand-washed and dried. If forks are soaked in this manner it is important to not let the forks soak for more than a few hours.

Individual salad forks come in two sizes, large and small. In some patterns salad forks are identified as pastry forks. Wallace currently labels its salad forks as 'Salad/Pastry Forks'. In an old Stieff catalog, the salad fork is identified as a 'Salad or Pastry Fork'. Gorham calls its current salad fork a 'Salad/Fish Fork'.

The small salad forks are also listed as small fish forks, and those in Figure 1.8 are classified as small fish forks or small salad forks. The example in *Strasbourg* is also labeled as a 'Small Pastry Fork'.

Figure 1.4, Salad Forks, Large: Gorham's *Strasbourg,*, 6 7/8"; *Lancaster,* 7"; *Rose Marie,* 6 5/8"; Whiting's *Louis XV,* 6 13/16"; and Jenkins and Jenkins' *Rose,* 6 5/8".

Salad Forks, Regular

Figure 1.5, Salad Forks, Regular:
Top row: Gorham's *La Scala*, 6 3/8"; *Chantilly*, 6"; Stieff's *Corsage*, 6 1/8"; Gorham's *King Edward*, 6 3/8"; Wallace's *Grand Colonial*, 6 3/8"; Gorham's *Buttercup*, 6 5/8"; Gorham's *Strasbourg*, 6 3/8"; and Durgin's *Dauphin*, 6 1/4".
Bottom row: Reed and Barton's *Hepplewhite*, 6 1/16"; *Marlborough*, 6 1/16"; *Francis I*, 6 1/8"; International's *Royal Danish*, 6 3/8"; Gorham's *Sovereign*, 6 9/16"; International's *Prelude*, 6 9/16"; and Towle's *King Richard*, 6 9/16".

Salad or Fish Forks, Small

Figure 1.6, Salad Fork, Small: Gorham's *Chantilly*, 6"; *Strasboourg*, 5 7/8"; and *Lancaster*, 5 1/16".

Fish Forks, Large

The fish fork is the next size fork in some patterns. The fish fork was created in response to requests from the people who had become accustomed to using fish forks and fish knives while traveling in Europe. Almost all European patterns have fish forks and fish knives available as well as related fish serving implements. The American versions of the fish fork were a large fork to compliment large dinner utensils and a smaller size for the luncheon utensils.

In the *Strasbourg* pattern by Gorham, the current salad fork is listed as a 'Salad/Fish Fork'. In the original items made in *Strasbourg* there were two sizes, a large size and a small size. The fork in some patterns is notable because of the double entry for the fork. An example of this is the pictured *Dauphin* fork which was labeled as a 'Fish Fork, Large' or a 'Small Cold Meat Fork' (see Cold Meat Forks, Figure 3.17). This double entry allowed the manufacturer to have one fork perform more than one function.

Currently some manufacturers use a sterling hollow handle and insert a stainless finding for the fork and knife. Kirk uses a sterling handle and a stainless finding for the knife, but a solid silver fork for the individual fish fork, which is different than the salad fork.

Figure 1.7, Fish Forks, Large: Whiting's *Louis XV*, 6 13/16"; Towle's *King Richard*, 7 7/8 (note the hollow handle); Gorham's *Strasbourg*, 7 1/2"; *Lancaster*, 7"; and Jenkins and Jenkins' *Rose*, 6 5/8".

Figure 1.8, Fish Fork, Small: Gorham's *Chantilly*, 6"; *Strasbourg*, 5 7/8"; and *Lancaster*, 5 1/16".

Dessert or Pastry Forks

Pastry forks, also known as dessert forks, are found in some patterns, but not in all. Each silver manufacturer made pastry forks, and each interpreted how this fork should look. Usually pastry forks had a bar connecting the tines, but this was not always the case. The pastry fork in Gorham's *Strasbourg* fills three jobs: it can also be called an 'Individual Fish Fork, Small' or an 'Individual Salad Fork, Small'. An old undated copy illustrating Gorham's *Buttercup* shows a 'Pickle or Pastry Fork'. The 1910-1911 Gorham catalog calls the same fork a 'Pickle Fork' only, another example of the changing names and assigned tasks of certain pieces. The second example shown in by Alvin is in its highly collectible pattern called *Orange Blossom*. It too has the bars between the tines. Currently *Orange Blossom* by Alvin, now a division of Gorham, is available in the Masterpiece Collection.

A list of items made in a pattern is truly a necessity. The pastry fork in Durgin's *Dauphin* is an example. Originally the *Dauphin* forks in Figure 1.9 were purchased as pie forks. Maryann Dolan's text, *1880s to 1990s American Sterling Flatware*, provided a number of lists for Durgin patterns. Among the patterns for which there were lists were *The Chatham, Cofax, DuBarry,* and *Fairfax*. Careful examination of the lists does not reveal a pie fork in any of these patterns. The only items listed were dessert or pastry forks, so the Durgin *Dauphin* forks must be dessert or pastry forks.

The two forks in Whiting's *Louis XV* are pastry forks. The first fork has small extensions on the outside tines. The second fork with the wide cutting tine qualifies it as a dessert/pastry fork.

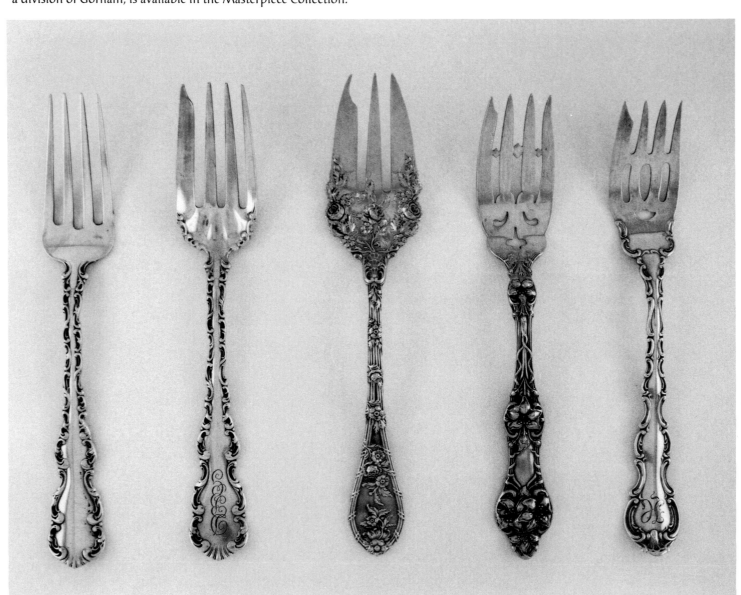

Figure 1.9, Pastry Forks: Whiting's *Louis XV*, 6 1/8", and 6 1/16"; Durgin's *Dauphin*, 6 1/8"; Alvin's *Old Orange Blossom*, 5 15/16"; and Gorham's *Strasbourg*, 5 7/8".

Pie Forks, Large

Pie forks were important to the Victorian table because meat or fruit filled pies were very popular. Because pies were even more common than salad, pie forks were created earlier than salad forks. Most pie forks came in two sizes. The *Rococco* pie fork by Dominick and Haff and the large *Lancaster* fork in Figure 1.10 illustrate the large sizes available when pie forks were popular.

Most of these forks had a wide cutting tine on the left side of the fork. This tine is a distinguishing feature. The large pie fork in Gorham's *Lancaster* typifies the large cutting tine. The smaller fork is sometimes identified as a pickle fork in some patterns. The small *Strasbourg* fork and the small *Lancaster* fork are the smaller versions of the pie fork.

Figure 1.10, Pie Fork, Large: Gorham's *Lancaster*, 7"; and Dominick and Haff's *Rococo*, 7 1/16".

Figure 1.11, Pie Fork, Small: Gorham's *Lancaster*, 5 13/16"; *Strasbourg*, 5 7/8"; Reed and Barton's *Hepplewhite*, 6"; *Louis XV*, 6 1/6"; unknown pattern, 6 7/8"; and Schofield's *Baltimore Rose*, 6 5/16".

Pickle Forks and Pickle Knives

Before refrigeration was common, wonderful fresh fruits and vegetables were not available throughout the year. During the summer cooks prepared or canned a large variety of pickles, relishes, chutneys, jams, and jellies for winter use. To sample and eat these, the pickle fork and knife were developed. Pickle forks were made in many patterns, as pickles were an important part of the diet, especially in the colder, northern parts of the United States. Pickle forks are usually identical to the small size pie fork in most Gorham patterns. The one catalog exception is in *Buttercup*, where an undated sheet shows the pickle or pastry fork as the same, though the 1910-1911 Gorham catalog does not do so. These forks can be substituted for salad forks in old sets without salad forks.

Figure 1.12, Pickle Forks and Knives: Whiting's *Louis XV*, fork, 6 3/8", and knife, 6 5/8"; Gorham's *Strasbourg*, fork, 5 7/8", and knife, 6 13/16"; *Lancaster*, fork, 5 13/16", and knife, 7 5/16"; Reed and Barton's *Hepplewhite*, fork, 6".

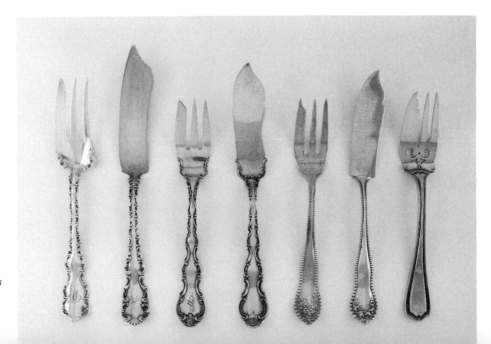

Junior Forks, Tea Forks, or Breakfast Forks

The breakfast fork was originally produced as part of a set for children to use. Its size was between baby-size silver and adult-size silver. Many adults soon realized that this mid-size fork and the rest of the set could be used at the breakfast table; thus, the items were sometimes labeled as breakfast forks. Some companies called the fork a tea fork, and it was accompanied by a tea knife. (See discussion of Breakfast Knives.)

Figure 1.13, Junior Forks, Tea Forks, or Breakfast Forks: Reed and Barton's *Pointed Antique*, 6 1/2"; Kirk's *Repoussé*, 6 5/16"; Towle's *King Richard*, 6 3/8"; Reed and Barton's *Francis I*, 5 21/32"; Gorham's *Buttercup*, 5 15/16"; Whiting's *Louis XV*, 6 1/8"; Reed and Barton's *Eighteenth Century*, 6 1/4"; Gorham's *Lancaster*, 5 15/16"; and Wallace's *Grand Colonial*, 5 11/16".

Bird Forks

Bird forks and Bird knives are hollow-handled items, usually found in pairs; however, the two examples shown in Figure 1.14 are without the accompanying knives. These items came into use with the tremendous amounts of game, notably birds that were served at one time in the United States. In Figure 1.14b a bird carving set is shown with a Haviland bird platter, an individual plate and an individual bird fork. These items are not seen frequently, and are rather rare.

Figure 1.14a, Bird Forks: Gorham's *Lancaster*, 6 1/2" and Whiting's *Louis XV*, 6 5/8".

Figure 1.14b, Bird Fork: Gorham's Lancaster individual bird fork, and a bird set— a serving fork, a serving knife, and a knife sharpener. *Photograph by David Reichard*

Lettuce Forks, Individual

Individual lettuce forks are found in few major patterns. The example in *Waverly* by Wallace is an exception, because *Waverly* was a full line pattern. A full line pattern consisted of flatware with both place and serving pieces made to match. The collector lucky enough to have a set of these forks would find them an interesting accompaniment to use for luncheons or even light salad meals.

Figure 1.15, Lettuce Fork, Individual: Wallace's *Waverly*, 6 1/8".

Ice Cream Forks, Large

Thomas Jefferson learned to enjoy ice cream while serving as ambassador to France, and introduced it to the United States while he was president. Ice cream was available during the winter months and as long as the ice stored from the winter lasted into summer. Making ice cream on a farm provided an opportunity to use extra cream that was not made into butter. Ice cream forks were made in two sizes, large and small. They were also called cake/ice cream forks, taking into account the short tines at the base of the fork. Ice cream and cake go together, and the fork is an effective utensil for eating them both.

Figure 1.16, Ice Cream Fork, Large: Towle's *King Richard*, 5 9/16"; Gorham's *Strasbourg*, 5 13/16"; Durgin's *Dauphin*, 5 7/8"; Gorham's *Lancaster*, 5 3/4"; and Whiting's *Louis XV*, 5 15/32".

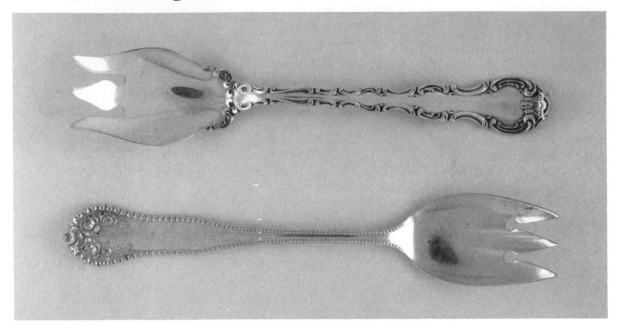

Figure 1.17, Ice Cream Fork, Small: Gorham's *Strasbourg*, 4 15/16"; and *Lancaster*, 5".

Cocktail Forks

Cocktail forks are used to stab and eat small pieces of seafood, often served in a sauce. Cocktail forks usually have three short tines at the end of a handle that is longer than a teaspoon's handle. These individual forks are set out for guests to use at the cocktail or hors d' oeuvres table. Sometimes a butter knife is paired with the cocktail fork to cut food into smaller pieces at the cocktail table.

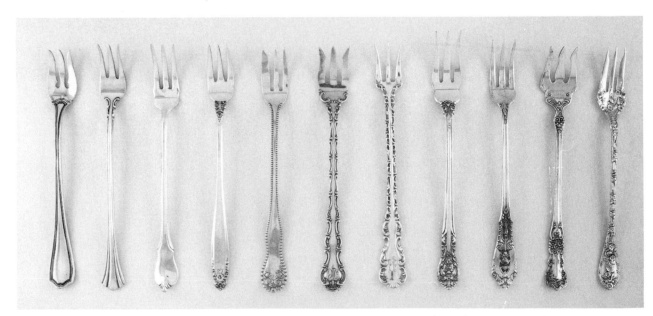

Figure 1.18, Cocktail Forks: Reed and Barton's *Hepplewhite*, 5 1/2"; *Eighteenth Century*, 5 19/32"; Wallace's *Grand Colonial*, 5 9/16"; International's *Prelude*, 5 1/2"; Gorham's *Lancaster*, 5 1/2"; *Strasbourg*, 5 7/16"; Whiting's *Louis XV*, 5 1/2"; Gorham's *King Edward*, 5 13/16"; Wallace's *Rose Point*, 5 5/8"; Gorham's *Buttercup*, 5 1/2"; and Durgin's *Dauphin*, 5 9/16".

Terrapin Forks

The development of terrapin forks is tied to the location of warm freshwater or tidewater turtles along the Gulf and Atlantic coasts, but not north of Massachusetts. Terrapin was a delicacy and was served as a separate course, usually in place of the fish course, and like other specialty foods, it required a specialized fork. Most terrapin forks have a round bowl with four short tines located on the bottom of the bowl. Terrapin forks can easily double as ice cream forks if ice cream forks are not available.

Figure 1.19, Terrapin Forks: Whiting's *Louis XV*, 5 3/8"; Durgin's *Dauphin*, 5 1/2"; and Gorham's *Strasbourg*, 5 1/32".

Ramekin Forks

Ramekin forks were made to be used with two part ramekin dish, consisting of a small ramekin cup and an underplate. The ramekin usually held a portion of some type of seafood in a very rich white sauce, and the underplate made passing or serving easier. The food was so rich that a very small serving was sufficient. Another recipe served in ramekin dishes, according to *Mrs. Beeton's Book of Household Management*, was chopped ham baked in a custard sauce. Ramekin forks were usually made in only the more popular patterns by the larger silver manufac-turers. While not exactly rare, they are not found with great regularity. Haviland produced ramekins and underplates for these specialized forks. Most ramekin forks were shorter than a cocktail fork but differed in the shape of the tines and bowl. The ramekin fork had four short tines and some piercing above the tines. Piercing below the handle is often found, especially in Gorham's patterns. Tiffany and Company made terrapin forks, but also cross-referenced them with ramekin forks and soufflé forks.

Figure 1.20, Ramekin Forks: Shreve's *Neapolitan*, 5 1/8"; Gorham's *Chesterfield*, 4 15/16"; Gorham's *Lancaster*, 5"; and Whiting's *Louis XV*, 5 1/16".

Strawberry Forks

The strawberry fork is the smallest fork and is truly a remnant of the bygone Victorian age. In the 1880s many improved strains of strawberries were introduced to the public and they were very well received because they were such an improvement over wild strawberries. Since most food had a specific implement it took little time for silver manufacturers to introduce a strawberry fork.

Strawberry forks usually have three tines, but some have only two tines (note Whiting's *Louis XV*). Some companies made two sizes, long and regular (or short). In some patterns the long-handled fork might be mistaken for a lemon fork, especially if the fork has the piercing above the tines which is characteristic of lemon forks (see Lemon Forks, Part III). Strawberry forks originally could be purchased as a berry set consisting of six forks and a berry spoon. Sets were also available without the berry spoon, and the forks were sold separately. Wallace, International, Towle, Reed and Barton, and Gorham have from time to time made strawberry forks, and these companies continue to produce them today. If a strawberry fork in a pattern that was introduced after 1930 is found at an antique show it most likely is one of the current items. Falling into this category are the following examples: Towle's *Old Master* and *King Richard*; Wallace's *Grand Baroque, Sir Christopher, Rosepoint,* and *Grand Colonial*; International's *Royal Danish* and *Joan of Arc*. These forks, even when new, are a delight to own and use. Collectors who wish to begin a sterling silver flatware collection can collect strawberry forks in some matching patterns, or collect various patterns in floral patterns or some other style. Older strawberry forks in the photograph numbered Figure 1.21 include the following: Gorham's *Chantilly, Strasbourg, Lancaster* and *Buttercup*; Dominic and Haff's *Mazarin* and *King Charles*; and Durgin's *Dauphin* and *Louis XV*.

Condiments served with strawberries might include regular cream, whipped cream, sour cream, brown sugar, powdered sugar, cinnamon, or plain powdered sugar. China manufacturers made a strawberry basket that included a small cream pitcher and a sugar bowl placed into the sides of the basket. Removing the creamer and sugar creates space for additional condiments.

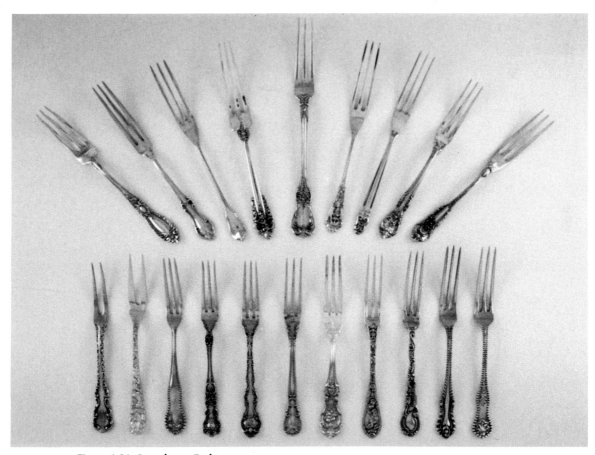

Figure 1.21, Strawberry Forks:
Top row: Towle's *King Richard*, 4 7/8"; International's *Joan of Arc*, 4 15/16"; Wallace's *Grand Colonial*, 5"; Wallace's *Grand Baroque*, 5 1/8"; Towle's *Old Master*, 5 5/8"; Wallace's *Rose Point*, 5"; International's *Royal Danish*, 5"; Gorham's *King Edward*, 4 11/16"; and Wallace's *Sir Christopher*, 4 13/16".
Bottom row: Whiting's *Louis XV*, 4 15/32"; Schofield's *Baltimore Rose*, 5"; Gorham's *Lancaster*, 4 9/16"; *Buttercup*, 4 9/16"; *Strasbourg*, 4 9/16"; *Chantilly*, 4 11/16"; Reed and Barton's *Francis I*, 4 13/16"; Durgin's *Dauphin*, 4 7/8"; *Louis XV*, 4 7/8"; Dominick and Haff's *Mazarin*, 5 1/16"; and *King Charles*, 5 12/16".

Lobster or Shellfish Forks

This particular fork, while resembling a cocktail fork, may be a lobster fork because it is flat, and the trident shape of the tines suggests seafood use. In Figure 1.22 the picture of the unusual *Louis XV* fork may be an example of a lobster fork.

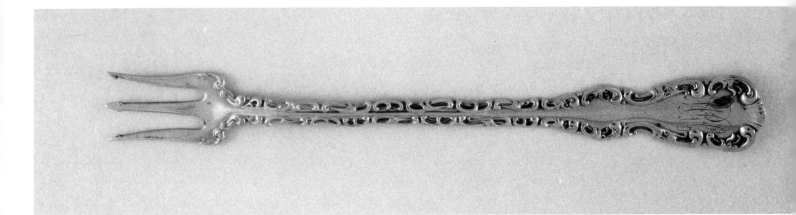

Figure 1.22, Lobster or Shellfish Fork: Whiting's *Louis XV*, 6 1/8".

Other forks that were made in some patterns, but unavailable for photographing were the following:

Cherry or Canapé Forks
Lobster Forks
Mango Forks
Melon Forks
Smelt Forks

Knives

Knives were the first pieces of silverware. They have been in use for a long time and have undergone some remarkable changes in size, use, and most importantly in the materials from which they are made. One positive outcome of World War II was the development of stainless steel, which has revolutionized the silver industry. Today knife blades are made of stainless steel that can go into a dishwasher, take a great deal of neglect, and still look good.

At first knives had blades that were made of silver-plated steel. These blades were fine for a while, but salt left spots which at times caused pitting, especially if the knives were not washed immediately. Other types of blades were made, but none proved totally successful. At one time Gorham offered plain steel blades and, for an additional fee, silver-plated blades. As these knives aged, the silver-plating on the cutting edge wore off and frequently the knife had a rusty edge. The early blades were usually blunt, but later styles were developed called French style, French style blunt, place size, and finally the modern style blade. During World War II the Grill Style was popular. It had elongated handles with short blades.

Knives come in dinner size, which is sometimes called 'place size, large' or 'table knife'. Next in decreasing size come place size knives with place size blades in modern or French style. Luncheon knives come next, with blunt blades in the French or modern styles. Some luncheon knives were made entirely of silver, and these were called 'all-silver dessert knives' or 'all-silver luncheon knives'. Fish knives were either all silver or hollow-handled, with either a sterling blade or a stainless blade that was inserted into the handle. Fruit knives were made with silver-plated bladews and later with stainless blades. Orange knives, either all silver or hollow-handled with a silver-plated blade, often have serrated edges. Butter knives come in a wide variety of shapes and sizes. Butter knives can be found as all-silver implements in as many as three sizes, or with stainless or sterling blades inserted into hollow handles. Other knives available in some patterns were steak knives, and junior, tea, or breakfast knives.

Dinner Knives

The largest size knife, the dinner size or place size, large comes with a variety of blades. Some old sets will be found with blunt blades, but later examples of knives have French style blades and new examples will have modern blades. The *Dauphin* examples in Figure 1.23 show a variety of blade styles made within that particular pattern. Other patterns also had a variety of blades.

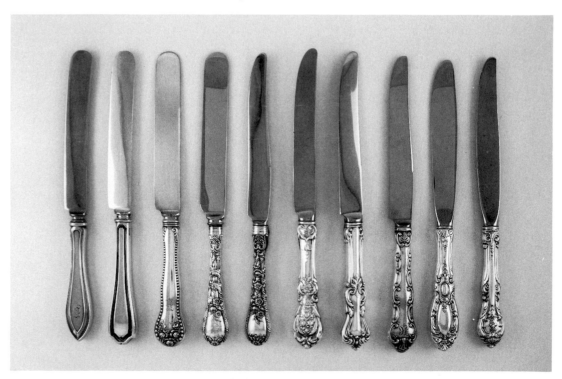

Figure 1.23, Dinner Knives, or Place Size, Large: Dominick and Haff's *Priscilla* (blunt), 9 5/8"; Reed and Barton's *Hepplewhite* (blunt), 9 5/8"; Gorham's *Lancaster* (blunt), 9 9/16"; Durgin's *Dauphin* (blunt), 9 1/2"; *Dauphin* (French), 9 1/2"; Reed and Barton's *Francis I* (French), 9 5/8"; *Marlborough* (French), 9 5/8"; Gorham's *Strasbourg* (French), 9 9/16"; Towle's *King Richard* (modern), 9 1/2"; and Gorham's *King Edward* (modern), 9 1/2".

Place Knives

The place knife is currently the most popular sized knife. It was developed after World War II as a cross between a large dinner knife and a too-small luncheon knife. It falls somewhere in between these two examples. These knives can be found with a variety of blade shapes and styles.

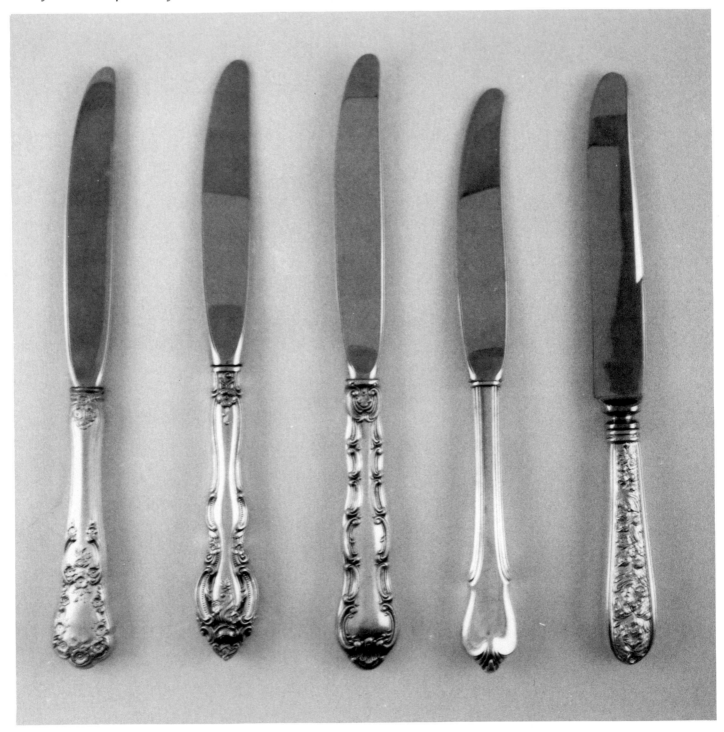

Figure 1.24, Place Knives: Gorham's *Buttercup*, 9 1/16"; *La Scala*, 9"; *Strasbourg*, 9 1/4"; Wallace's *Grand Colonial*, 8 3/4"; and Stieff's *Corsage*, 9".

Luncheon or Dessert Knives, Hollow-Handled

The luncheon knife is a small knife and when paired with a luncheon fork it can be used whenever a knife is needed, not just for luncheons. They probably evolved because women found the dinner-size knife too difficult to manage. Luncheon knives can be found with a large variety of blade styles, from blunt to French-style. If you are trying to match a particular style or shape of blade, it is wise to carry photocopies of the silver you are attempting to match. Silver photocopies beautifully, and it is simpler to carry a sheet of paper than all those samples.

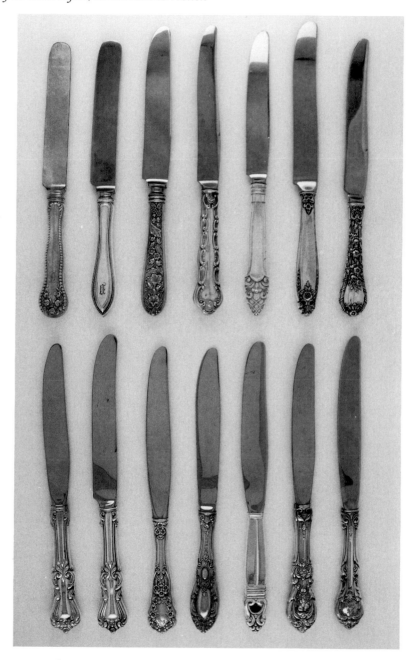

Figure 1.25, Luncheon Knives or Dessert Knives:
Top row: Gorham's *Lancaster* (blunt), 9 1/8"; Dominick and Haff's *Priscilla* (blunt), 8 1/2". (The following knives all have French-style blades): Stieff's *Corsage*, 8 7/8"; Gorham's *Strasbourg*, 8 7/8"; *Sovereign*, 8 13/16"; International's *Prelude*, 9 1/16"; and Durgin's *Dauphin*, 8 17/32".
Bottom row: Reed and Barton's *Marlborough* (modern), 8 7/8"; *Marlborough* (French), 9 1/8". (The following knives in the row all have modern blades): Gorham's *Buttercup*, 8 3/4"; Towle's *King Richard*, 8 5/8"; International's *Royal Danish*, 8 7/8"; Reed and Barton's *Francis I*, 8 13/16"; and Gorham's *King Edward*, 8 15/16".

Luncheon or Dessert Knives, Flat, All Silver

All-silver luncheon or dessert knives were made in only a few patterns. Gorham, in an old brochure describing its made-to-order program, notes that in the pattern *Cluny*, only hand-cast knives will be supplied. These would be the all-silver knives. (For examples in *Cluny*, see Ice Cream Servers in Figure 3.43). The example in Gorham's *Strasbourg* is truly representative of the all-silver dessert knife. This knife helps set a beautiful table.

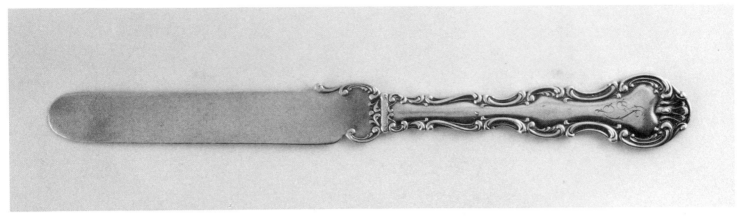

Figure 1.26, Luncheon Knives or Dessert Knives, All Silver: Gorham's *Strasbourg*, 7 27/32".

Steak Knives

The introduction of the steak knife made the cutting of meat easier. Most steak knives have excellent cutting blades inserted into sterling handles. Many of the steak blades or findings come from England or Germany. In some patterns no steak knives were made while the pattern was manufactured. More recently, however, enterprising antique dealers have produced steak knives by removing old blades and setting new steak blades into antique sterling handles. Another possible explanation for finding steak knives in old patterns is that once a year manufacturers had made-to-order programs and possibly produced these knives. Regardless of age, steak knives are a joy to use and an asset to the collector fortunate enough to have them.

Figure 1.27, Steak Knife: Towle's *King Richard*, 8 5/8"; Gorham's *King Edward*, 9 3/16"; *Crown Baroque*, 9 3/4"; Reed and Barton's *Eighteenth Century*, 9 5/8"; and International's *Royal Danish*, 8 5/16".

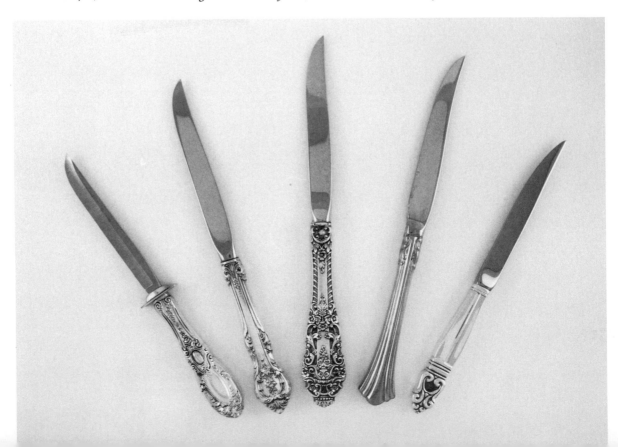

Fish Knives

Fish knives come in a variety of sizes, shapes, and materials. Some are hollow-handled with either a stainless blade or a sterling blade. Others are all silver which allows the manufacturer to place the design along the blade. Fish knives and fish forks can be used to stretch a sterling service by giving men one size of knives and forks, and the women the fish knives and forks. The two are excellent for use at a salad luncheon. Stieff and Company in an old brochure lists one of their items as a Butter Knife or a Fish Knife. In the photograph, Figure 1.28 the all silver examples in *Louis XV* show flat knives in both the large and small sizes. The sample in Durgin's *Dauphin* is the large all-silver fish knife. The hollow-handled fish knives in Towle's *King Richard* and Gorham's *Strasbourg* are representative of this style.

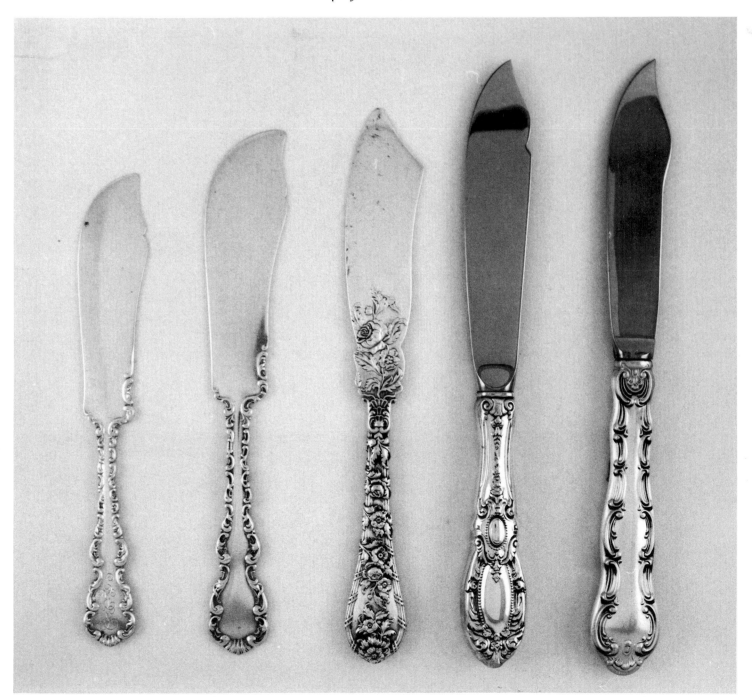

Figure 1.28, Fish Knives: (all silver) Whiting's *Louis XV*, 7 5/16" and 6 9/16", and Durgin's *Dauphin*, 7 5/8"; (hollow-handled, stainless steel blade) Towle's *King Richard*, 8 3/8"; and Gorham's *Strasbourg*, 8 5/8".

Junior Knives, Tea Knives, or Breakfast Knives

A special knife was developed to be used as an in-between size silver for children too old for baby silver and too young for adult size silver. Soon a loyal audience of adults developed who preferred using them at the breakfast table. Reed and Barton made tea knives and youth knives, giving each one a different blade. Youth knives or breakfast knives generally have modern-style blades, while tea knives have French blades. In the photograph, however, the *Pointed Antique* example with a French blade is nonetheless a youth knife. The examples in *Eighteenth Century*, *Francis I*, *Repoussé*, and *Grand Colonial* have modern blades. The *Louis XV* examples are all silver. The last example, in Gorham's *Lancaster*, is silver-plated and blunt.

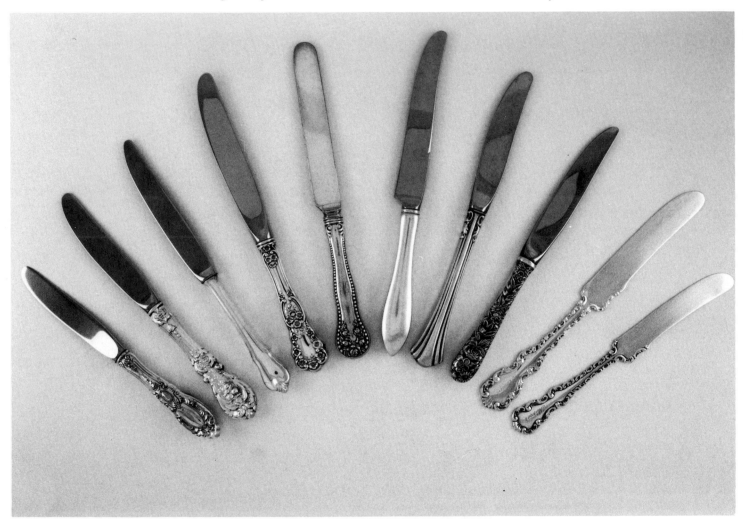

Figure 1.29, Tea Knives, Youth Knives, or Junior Knives: Towle's *King Richard*, 6 1/4"; Reed and Barton's *Francis I*, 7"; Wallace's *Grand Colonial*, 7 1/2"; Gorham's *Buttercup*, 7 1/2"; *Lancaster*, 7 9/16"; Reed and Barton's *Pointed Antique*, 7 21/32"; *Eighteenth Century*, 7 7/32"; Kirk's *Repoussé*, 7 3/16"; Whiting's (all silver) *Louis XV*, 7 3/32" and 6 1/2".

Fruit Knives

Fruit knives were made using sterling hollow handles with a plated blade or a stainless steel blade. These knives, when paired with sterling salad forks, make excellent sets for eating fruit desserts such as chocolate-coated poached pears. Some manufacturers, including Kirk and Sons, made specific fruit forks and knives. Many old individual sets of fruit forks and fruit knives can be found in plated silver, usually manufactured in Europe. The three examples in Figure 1-30 were made by Gorham in *Buttercup*, *Lancaster*, and *Strasbourg*. They are typical of fruit knives made in the United States.

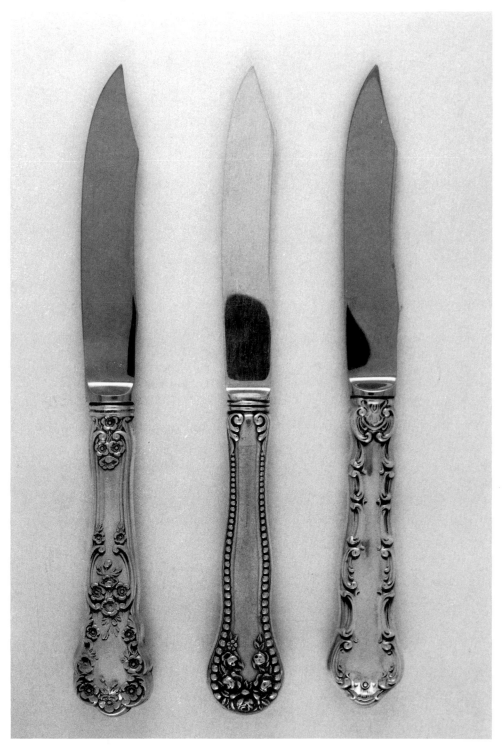

Figure 1.30, Fruit Knives: Gorham's *Buttercup*, 6 13/16"; *Lancaster*, 6 13/16"; *Strasbourg*, 6 13/16".

Butter Spreaders, Hollow-Handled

The butter spreader is usually the smallest individual knife. This knife is made in all silver in two or three sizes, depending upon the manufacturer. Hollow-handled knives with sterling or stainless blades were also made. A butter plate may be present on a formally set dining table, but it should be without a butter knife. Many people do not follow this rule, since butter knives seem to be a necessity, not a nuisance. Among the many examples in Figure 1.32 the all-silver blades and handles on Towle's *King Richard*, Gorham's *Sovereign*, and International's *Royal Danish* are unique. The three sizes in Whiting's *Louis XV* in Figure 1.33 are also different. The owner of the Whiting pieces special-ordered spreaders in the large size during a made-to-order promotion, but Gorham sent the extra long samples, thus adding other variations to a growing collection.

Figure 1.31, Butter Spreaders, Hollow-Handled: Reed and Barton's *Marlborough*, paddle-shaped blade, 6 3/16"; Modern (As found on all the remainder of these items), *Marlborough*, 6 7/16"; Gorham's *La Scala*, 6 1/2"; *Strasbourg*, 6 1/8"; *Decor*, 6 5/16"; *Buttercup*, 6 1/4"; *Lancaster*, 6 1/4"; and Wallace's *Grand Colonial*, 6 3/16.

Other knives that were made in some patterns, but unavailable for photographing include the following:

Crawfish Knife
Duck Knife
Melon Knife

For information on the Pickle Knife, refer to Pickle Forks and Pickle Knives, Figure 1-12.

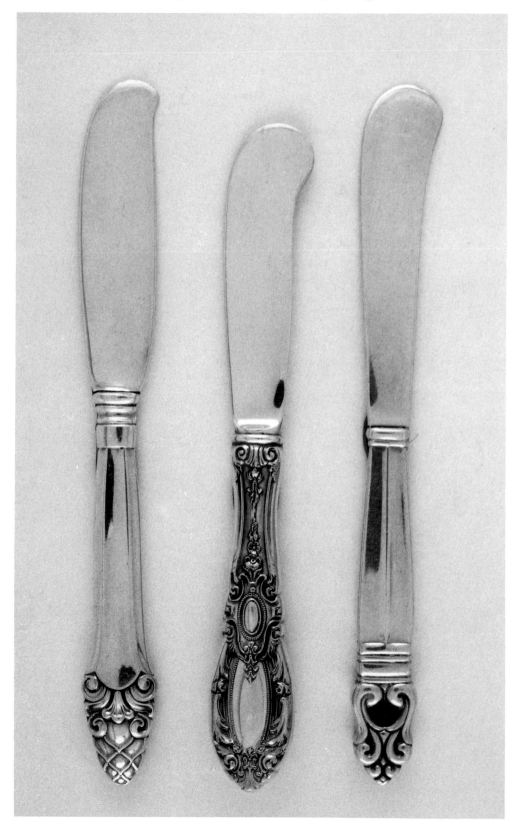

Figure 1.32, Butter Spreaders, All-silver Hollow-Handled: Gorham's *Sovereign*, 6"; Towle's *King Richard*, 5 11/16"; and International's *Royal Danish*, 6"

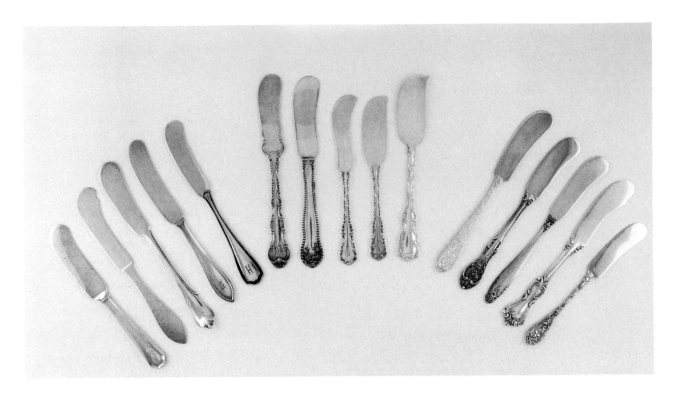

Figure 1.33, Butter Spreaders, Flat, All Silver: Gorham's *Fairfax*, 5 7/16"; (probably) Shreve's *Buckingham*, hand-hammered, 5 11/16"; Wallace's *Grand Colonial*, 6 1/16"; Dominick and Haff's *Priscilla*, 5 7/8"; Reed and Barton's *Hepplewhite*, 5 5/8"; Gorham's *Strasbourg*, 5 15/16"; *Lancaster*, 5 7/8"; Whiting's *Louis XV*, 5 7/8", 5", and 5 11/16"; Stieff's *Corsage*, 5 15/16"; Gorham's *King Edward*, 5 13/16"; International's *Prelude*, 5 13/16"; Reed and Barton's *Marlborough*, 5 15/16"; and Durgin's *Dauphin*, 5 1/4".

Orange Knives

Orange knives were made in some patterns. Some have sterling handles and serrated blades, and others are all silver with a serrated edge plus a pick at the end of the blade to pick up the fruit. In the Victorian home, these knives were considered a necessity. Silver-plate manufacturers also made special dishes to hold half of an orange or grapefruit. The all-silver sample in Durgin's *Louis XV* and the sterling hollow-handled knife in Gorham's *Lancaster* in Figure 1.34 are typical of this type of utensil.

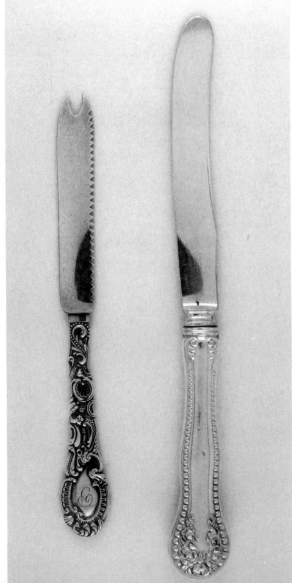

Figure 1.34, Orange Knives: Durgin's *Louis XV*, 5 7/8" and Gorham's *Lancaster*, 7 3/8".

Spoons

In this section the spoons have been arranged in order of size and are presented from the longest spoon to the shortest. The shape and length are specifically related to the type of food for which they are to be used. Thirteen different categories are presented, and some categories have more than one example embedded within the text.

Iced Tea Spoons

The longest individual spoon is usually the iced tea spoon, used to stir sugar into cool, refreshing iced tea. These spoons are long-handled, with a bowl at the end that is sometimes slightly smaller than a regular teaspoon bowl. The iced tea spoon can be found in two lengths in some patterns. The only true short-handled iced tea spoon is the spoon in *Louis XV*. The *Hepplewhite* iced tea spoon is shorter than the other sampled iced tea spoons, but published lists of *Hepplewhite* do not list it as a short iced tea spoon. Iced tea spoons are a regular item in place settings sold in the southern part of the United States, replacing cream soup spoons in the place setting.

A variation of the iced tea spoon is the muddler spoon, which was made only by the Kirk Company. The muddler spoon was used for mint juleps. It had a small oval bowl and at the end of the long spoon handle was a knob-like affair that was used to bruise the mint leaves. The French made a similar spoon and called it a *cuiller a verre d'eau*. This translates literally to "spoon for a glass of water." These French spoons may have been used to scrape sugar from a cone or to bruise lemon peel to flavor water. A Kirk designer may have traveled to France and seen the French spoons; then he returned home and designed the American version. The iced teaspoon and the muddler spoon are pictured in Figure 1.35 and readers can compare how similar they are.

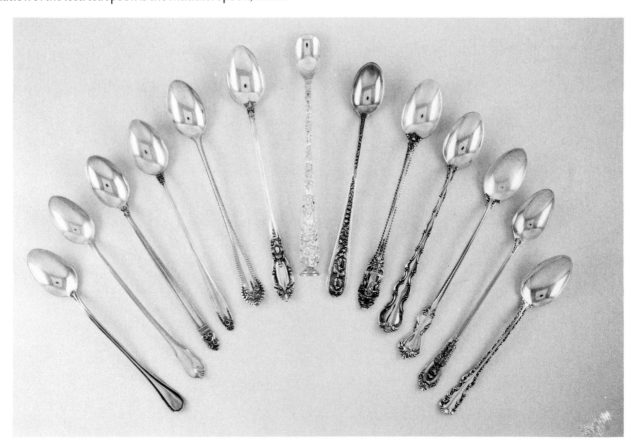

Figure 1.35, Iced Tea Spoons: Reed and Barton's *Hepplewhite*, 7"; Wallace's *Grand Colonial*, 7 1/2"; International's *Royal Danish*, 7 5/16"; *Prelude*, 7 5/16"; Gorham's *Lancaster*, 7 1/2"; Towle's *King Richard*, 8 3/16"; Kirk's *Repoussé* Muddler, 7 11/16"; Stieff's *Corsage*, 7 7/16"; Gorham's *Crown Baroque*, 7 9/16"; *Strasbourg*, 7 1/2"; Reed and Barton's *Marlborough*, 7 7/8"; Wallace's *Rose Point*, 7 5/8"; and Whiting's *Louis XV*, 6 3/4".

Dessert Spoons

The dessert spoon is the correct spoon at a formal dinner for eating soup. The correct china piece to use for soup is a soup plate —approximately the size of a dinner plate, less than two inches tall, and usually rimmed. Rimmed pieces are more formal than rimless ones. The dessert spoons shown in Figure 1.36 all have basically the same shape. Dessert spoons are midway in size between a teaspoon and a tablespoon with basically the same shape.

Figure 1.36, Dessert Spoons: Whiting's *Louis XV*, 6 7/8"; Durgin's *Dauphin*, 7 3/32"; Towle's *King Richard*, 7 1/4"; Gorham's *Lancaster*, 7"; Wallace's *Grand Colonial*, 6 15/16"; and Gorham's *Strasbourg*, 7".

Place Spoons

A place spoon is a cross between a cream soup spoon and a dessert spoon. Most silver companies introduced this item so that customers could purchase one spoon that could be used for both courses. It is slightly shorter, and somewhat more oval in the shape of the bowl than a dessert spoon. In Figure 1-37 three examples of place spoons from Gorham are the following: *La Scala*, *Crown Baroque*, and *King Edward*. Reed and Barton's *Eighteenth Century* is slightly larger than the Gorham spoons, yet they all share the same general shape.

Figure 1.37, Place Spoons: Gorham's *La Scala*, 6 5/8"; Reed and Barton's *Eighteenth Century*, 6 7/8"; *Crown Baroque*, 6 7/16"; and Gorham's *King Edward*, 6 3/4".

Large Round Bowl Soup Spoons

The large round bowl soup spoon is used for eating stews or soups (though these pieces can easily be used as serving spoons for Chinese take-out meals as well). Large round bowl spoons were usually manufactured in older patterns, and can be found with some diligent searching. Some silver dealers refer to this spoon as a 'Chowder Spoon'.

Figure 1.38, Large Round Bowl/Cream Soup Spoons: Whiting's *Louis XV*, 6 3/4"; Reed and Barton's *Hepplewhite*, 7 1/16"; Alvin's *Old Orange Blossom*, 6 7/8"; Dominick and Haff's *Priscilla*, 7 1/4"; and Gorham's *Lancaster*, 6 3/4".

Cream Soup Spoons

Another soup spoon, the cream soup spoon, is usually paired with a cream soup cup and saucer to serve thick and creamy soups. This spoon is a standard item in a six piece place setting in most of the United States, though not in the South, where the iced tea spoon is the fifth member in a place setting. Most cream soup spoons have a round bowl, and a handle that is longer than a teaspoon handle. An exception to this is the cream soup spoon in Reed and Barton's patterns such as *Marlboro.*, which have shorter handles than other cream soup spoons do. Readers should refer to Figure 2.5, which shows the three types of soup spoons manufactured and the correct corresponding china piece to use. The three types of soup spoons are the bouillon spoon, the cream soup and the dessert or formal soup spoon.

Figure 1.39, Cream Soup Spoons: Wallace's *Grand Colonial*, 6"; Towle's *King Richard*, 6 1/16"; Reed and Barton's *Marlborough*, 5 3/4"; International's *Royal Danish*, 6 1/2"; Gorham's *Buttercup*, 6 1/4"; International's *Prelude*, 6 1/4"; Gorham's *Sovereign*, 6 5/16"; *Strasbourg*, 6 1/8"; and *King Edward*, 6 1/4".

Sorbet Spoons

Sorbet spoons are made in some of the most popular patterns, but even so they are not very plentiful. A small serving of sorbet, which is a small iced dessert item made in an ice cream machine, is served between courses to cleanse the palate or as light dessert finale to a heavy dinner.

Figure 1.40, **Sorbet Spoon:** Whiting's *Louis XV*, 5 7/8".

Parfait Spoons

Parfait spoons, with their egg-shaped bowls, were designed for eating ice cream desserts layered with fruit and sauce and served in parfait glasses. Most were produced by either the flatware manufacturers Stieff or Kirk. Parfait spoons can be substituted for ice cream spoons and used at luncheons.

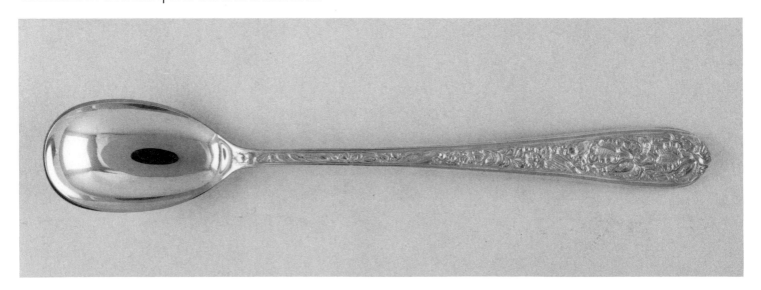

Figure 1.41, **Parfait Spoon:** Stieff's *Corsage*, 5 7/8".

Ice Cream Spoons, Large

Victorian homes often had ice cream spoons in large and/or small sizes. Most ice cream spoons can be identified by comparison with a teaspoon—ice cream spoons are usually smaller and may have a fancy bowl. These spoons were developed when ice cream became a popular dessert. If cake is served with the ice cream, ice cream forks were used. Ice cream spoons are great to use for eating sundaes with various sauces and nuts topped with whipped cream.

Figure 1.42, Ice Cream Spoons, Large: Durgin's *Dauphin,* 5 3/4"; Gorham's *Cluny,* 6 1/16"; Whiting's *Louis XV,* 5 13/16"; Gorham's *Lancaster,* 5 3/8".

Figure 1.43, Ice Cream Spoons, Small: Gorham's *Baronial*, 5"; Whiting's *Louis XV*, 5 1/8; Gorham's *Strasbourg*, 5 1/4"; and Wallace's *Rose*, 5 1/4"

Teaspoons

The teaspoon is a common piece of silver flatware. Teaspoons were developed as a necessary implement for drinking tea, which was introduced into England about 1600 and became part of daily life in the American colonies by 1700. When tea was first introduced to Europe the tea leaves were eaten, but after learning more about tea, people used teaspoons to remove floating tea leaves and to stir the sugar and cream into the tea.

Many implements were developed to use in serving and drinking tea. The tea caddy spoon, for example, was used to remove an amount of tea for brewing from a locked tea caddy box. Other utensils were the tea strainer, the tea ball, and the tea ball teaspoon or infuser. The tea ball spoon was a teaspoon with a hinged lid (Gorham called its item a Tea Maker) that held the tea leaves while the tea brewed. For a further discussion of tea items, see Miscellaneous at the end of this section.

Many people purchase twice as many teaspoons as other forks and knives, especially if their pattern is new and fewer specialty items are available from which to choose. Teaspoons can be used for any of the specialized spoons, parfait, ice cream, or even sorbet. Having extra teaspoons allows one to be used for dessert, and another for coffee or tea.

Figure 1.44, Teaspoons:
Top row: Alvin's *Bridal Rose*, 5 7/8"; International's *Frontenac*, 5 13/16"; Towle's *Georgian*, 5 7/8"; Gorham's *Old Medici*, 5 29/32"; and Durgin's *Chrysanthemum*, 5 3/4".
Middle row: Gorham's *Lyric*, 5 7/8"; Lunt's *Monticello*, 5 11/16"; Tiffany's *Marquise*, 5 13/16"; Lunt's *William and Mary*, 6"; Gorham's *Jefferson*, 5 3/4"; and Wallace's *Grand Baroque*, 6 1/8".
Bottom row: Durgin's *New Queens*, 5 13/16"; Alvin's, *Orange Blossom*, 5 13/16"; Reed and Barton's *Marlborough*, 5 13/16"; Gorham's *Decor*, 5 7/8"; and Watson's *Pine Cone*, 5 15/16".

Pap Spoons

Pap spoons were made for feeding pap, a thin ground wheat cereal, to invalids. These spoons were made in many patterns, and the item shown in *Louis XV* is an example. It has a narrow, upturned end, which would certainly be helpful in feeding someone who was very ill. Spoons made by other companies have bowls in the shape of a small dessert spoon bowl, and shorter handles.

Figure 1.45, **Pap Spoons:** Whiting's *Louis XV*, 5 3/4".

Chocolate Spoons, Long-Handled

In the 1800s, hot chocolate drinks were served in specially-designed chocolate cups. Much less refined than it is today, the chocolate of the late nineteenth century required constant stirring to keep it from settling to the bottom of the cup, prompting the development of the chocolate spoon.

The examples in the photograph show three variations of the chocolate spoon within the *Dauphin* pattern. Long-handled spoons were used for tall chocolate cups, regular spoons with the bowl matching the chocolate muddler for regular cups, and even a round bowl spoon also for regular cups. It is interesting to see that Durgin changed the shape of the chocolate spoon sometime during the production run of *Dauphin*.

Today chocolate spoons can be used to eat mousse or rich pudding dessert, or for their original purpose.

Figure 1.46, **Chocolate Spoons, Long-Handled:**
Top row: Gorham's *Lancaster*, 4 3/4".
Bottom row: Durgin's *Dauphin*, 5 7/16".

Figure 1.47, Chocolate Spoons, Short-Handled: Durgin's *Dauphin* (tipped end), 4 7/32"; Whiting's *Louis XV*, 4 1/32"; Durgin's *Dauphin* (round bowl), 4 3/16"; Gorham's *Lancaster*, 4 1/16" and *Cambridge*, 4 1/8".

Citrus Spoons (Grapefruit, Orange & Melon)

Citrus spoons, sometimes called grapefruit or orange spoons, were developed to serve citrus fruits during the early 1890s. At that time there was a tremendous citrus crop and silver manufacturers teamed up with the citrus industry to offer a number of unique silver items for use with citrus fruit at the table.

Some companies made separate spoons to serve each citrus fruit, while others made only one spoon. The only way to tell whether a particular spoon is a grapefruit, orange, or citrus spoon for certain is to check a copy of the design patent for the name; otherwise, call the spoon a citrus spoon. Gorham calls their spoon a "Grapefruit or Melon" spoon. In Figure 1.49 the example in *Lancaster* is an orange spoon. The grapefruit spoon has a slight lip making is just a shade wider than the orange spoon. An old brochure from Stieff labels their spoon as "Grapefruit or Orange Spoons." Wallace makes this spoon today and calls it a Grapefruit Spoon. Some of the spoons have gold-washed bowls; others do not.

Today citrus spoons can be used for eating fresh melons as well as citrus fruits. These spoons are sturdy and make it easy to separate the fruit from the surrounding tough membranes.

Figure 1.48, Citrus Spoons: Whiting's *Louis XV*, 5 3/8'; Gorham's *Lancaster*, 5 3/4"; Towle's *King Richard*, 5 7/8"; Durgin's *Dauphin*, 5 13/16"; Wallace's *Grand Colonial*, 5 7/16"; Gorham's *Strasbourg*, 5 5/8"; and Whiting's *Esther*, 5 9/16".

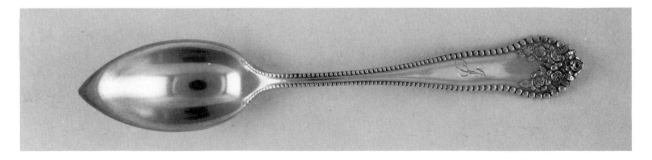

Figure 1.49, Orange Spoon: Gorham's *Lancaster*, 5 11/16".

Five O'Clock Spoons

Five o'clock teaspoons are smaller than regular teaspoons but larger than demitasse spoons. The name most likely came from being used at afternoon tea, close to five o'clock. In addition to use at the tea table, these teaspoons are the third piece of a youth or breakfast set. They are the right size for young children.

Figure 1.50, Five O'Clock Teaspoons: Reed and Barton's *Intaglio*, 5 5/16"; *Francis I*, 5 7/16"; Gorham's *Lancaster*, 5 5/16"; Reed and Barton's *Pointed Antique*, 5 3/8"; Kirk's *Repoussé*, 5 7/16"; Whiting's *Louis XV*, 5 1/4"; Gorham's *Buttercup*, 5 7/16"; Wallace's *Grand Colonial*, 5 5/16"; and Towle's *King Richard*, 5 1/2".

Bouillon Spoons

Bouillon spoons are another implement for eating soup. Bouillon is a clear broth that is served in bouillon cups, usually at the start of a formal dinner. Most bouillon spoons have a round bowl on a short handle, which is difficult for many people to hold. The *Dauphin* bouillon spoon handles are relatively long compared to the *Strasbourg* spoons. One reason for this may be that Durgin did not make a cream soup spoon and the longer handle made the spoon usable both as a cream soup spoon and a bouillon spoon. Another advantage to this longer handle is that it is easier to hold.

The comparison of the various types of spoons and the accompanying china can be seen in Figure 2.10. Most bouillon cups are basically the same shape as coffee cups, but have two handles. The cream soup cup has a larger bowl than a bouillon cup and rests on an underplate. The large rim soup, the correct size for a formal dinner, is pictured with a dessert spoon, the correct soup spoon for a formal dinner. These items are pictured in Part II, in the section discussing *Strasbourg* and in Figure 2.10.

Figure 1.51, Bouillon Spoons: Durgin's *Dauphin*, 5 11/16"; Towle's *King Richard*, 5 7/16"; Gorham's *Lancaster*, 5 1/8"; Shreve's *Buckingham* (hand-hammered), 5 1/8"; Gorham's *Strasbourg*, 5 3/32"; and Dominick and Haff's *Priscilla*, 5 3/8"; and Whiting's *Louis XV*, 5".

Egg Spoons

Eggs were an important part of breakfast in Victorian homes and specialized spoons and cups were commonly used to eat boiled eggs served in the shell. Most egg spoons have elongated bowls on a rather short handle, and some have a chicken motif worked into the design, or on the reverse of the spoon. Many were gold-washed to help prevent tarnishing when coming in contact with the egg yolk.

At one time the silver manufacturers produced a silver-plated egg cooker, which called for the use of egg spoons, and Tiffany even made a sterling egg cooker! The illustration in Figure 1.52b shows an English Combination Toast Rack and Egg Cup Holder. Egg spoons were made in a variety of old patterns and can be found from time to time. Many older china patterns continue to make egg cups available for purchase today.

Figure 1.52a, Egg Spoons: Gorham's *Buttercup*, 5"; Reed and Barton's *Medallion* (patented December 24, 1868), 6 3/16"; and Gorham's *Lancaster*, 5".

Figure 1.52b, Egg Spoons: all in Gorham's *Buttercup*.

Demitasse Spoons

Demitasse spoons closely resemble miniature teaspoons. Today they can be used to serve rich desserts like chocolate mousse from delicate old demitasse cups or chocolate cups.

Collectors enjoy collecting demitasse spoons because they are readily available at antique shows and are relatively inexpensive. Collectors can assemble a large number of patterns or they can concentrate on particular styles. Like salt spoons, demitasse spoons provide a stimulus for lagging dinner conversations.

Figure 1.53, Demitasse or Coffee Spoons:
Top row: Gorham's *Crown Baroque*, 4 7/16"; Kirk's *Old Maryland Engraved*, 4 1/8"; Gorham's *Chantilly*, 4 1/8"; Towle's *King Richard*, 4 1/2"; *Old Master*, 5 3/16"; Durgin's *Dauphin*, 4 3/16"; Reed and Barton's *Eighteenth Century*, 4 1/4"; Gorham's *Number Eighteen*, 4 1/16"; *Repoussé*, 4 1/4"; Gorham's *Strasbourg*, 3 29/32"; and International's *Richeleau*, 4 1/8".
Bottom row: Towle's *Candlelight*, 4 3/8"; Gorham's *King Edward*, 4 3/16"; *Lily of the Valley*, 4 5/8"; Towle's *Rambler Rose*, 4 3/8"; Reed and Barton's *Hepplewhite*, 4 3/16"; Wallace's *Grand Colonial*, 4 1/16"; Gorham's *Buttercup*, 4 1/8"; *Cambridge*, 4 1/8"; and Whiting's *Lily of the Valley*.

Salt Spoons

The smallest spoon is the individual salt spoon, meant to accompany individual salt dishes. The individual salt spoon usually has a round bowl on a short two to three inch handle. Most manufacturers have made these tiny spoons available in their patterns at some time. Neophyte collectors might want to begin their collections with salt spoons because they are easily found at antique shows and they are relatively inexpensive.

Figure 1.54, Salt Spoon, Individual:
Top row: Gorham's *Lancaster*, 2 11/16"; Whiting's *Louis XV*, 2 1/4"; *Grand Colonial*, 2 7/16"; Kirk's *Repoussé*, 2 3/8"; Wallace's *Grand Colonial*, 2 7/16"; Gorham, unknown pattern, 2 3/4"; and Kirk's *Repoussé*, 2 3/8".
Bottom row: Gorham's *King Edward*, 2 13/16"; Stieff's *Rose*, 2 7/8"; Gorham, unknown pattern, 2 7/16"; Stieff's *Corsage*, 2 7/8"; and Gorham's *Strasbourg*, 2 13/16".

Children's Silver

All forms of children's silver can be seen in this figure: the infant feeding spoon, the baby set, the food pusher, and the three-piece youth set. The food pusher is introduced about the time the child begins using the baby set. The three-piece set can be used as breakfast silver after the child is finished with the set.

Figure 1.55, Children's Silver: all in Gorham's *Buttercup.* Infant feeding spoon, 5 5/16"; baby fork, 4 1/2"; baby spoon, 4 1/2"; food pusher, 4"; youth fork, 5 15/16"; youth knife, 7 1/2"; and youth spoon, 5 1/2".

Baby Sets

A child's introduction to silver usually begins with an infant feeding spoon (See bottom of Figure 1.56). Infant feeding spoons are graceful spoons used for feeding formula and pureed food to a baby. After the child outgrows the spoon, it can be used for parfait, or for serving olives and relishes. Infant feeding spoons are a gift that a child can use throughout a lifetime. When the spoons are engraved and monogrammed they can be even more important. Eventually the spoons can be passed down from parent to child or grandchild.

After the infant feeding spoon, the child gradually works to or grows into the two-piece baby set (See top of Figure 1.56). The set consists of a large bowl spoon and a fork, both on short handles designed to fit the hand of a young child.

Figure 1.56, Baby and Infant Silver:
Top row, Baby Silver: Reed and Barton, *Eighteenth Century*, spoon, 4 9/16", and fork, 4 9/16"; Gorham, *Buttercup*, spoon, 4 1/2", and fork, 4 1/2"; *Greenbriar*, spoon, 4 9/16", and fork, 4 9/16".
Bottom row, Infant Feeding Spoons: Towle's *Old Master*, 4 7/8"; Stieff's *Rose*, 5 5/8"; Kirk's *Repoussé*, 5 11/16"; *Old Maryland Engraved*, 5 11/16"; Gorham's *Buttercup*, 5 5/16"; Wallace's *Grand Baroque*, 5 5/8"; Reed and Barton's *Eighteenth Century*, 5 3/4"; Wallace's *Rose Point*, 5 5/8"; and Reed and Barton's *Pointed Antique*, 5 9/16".

Children's Silver & Youth Silver

The collection in Figure 1.57 includes children's silver forks and a spoon. Knives will be discussed and shown in Figure 1.58.

The first example at the top of Figure 1.57 is by Durgin, but the name of the pattern is unknown. Checking references and examples of Durgin's patterns produced no photographic clue, but the name of the pattern *Strawberry*, 1874, was all that was found in the *Sterling Flatware Pattern Index*. This then may be a first example of this lovely pattern.

Another noteworthy example also appears in this figure. The first fork on the bottom row made by Kirk is very interesting. The photograph appears to have a circular mark on the end of the fork, but close inspection reveals that the spot is where someone held the fork repeatedly; the tines show wear as well. Tines on forks that are well used usually become rounded; that is, the end tines are slightly shorter than the interior tines because the end tines usually are the first to pierce the food to be eaten and suffer the greater wear.

Figure 1.57, Children's Silver and Youth Silver:
Top row: Durgin's *Strawberry*, baby fork, 3 1/2"; Kirk's *Repoussé*, baby fork, 3 3/4"; *Rose*, baby spoon, 3 3/4"; *Repoussé*, 3 11/16"; and an unknown pattern (matches a food pusher in Figure 1.60), 3 3/16".
Bottom row: Early Kirk's youth fork (Marked 10.15), 5 11/16"; *Repoussé*, youth fork, 5 7/8"; Schofield's *Baltimore Rose*, Youth Fork, 4 5/8"; Jenkins and Jenkins, 4 7/16".

Children's Knives

These three examples show the variety of knives that have been produced for children. The first example, Kirk's *Repoussé* is all silver and is of a mid-sized length. Stieff's *Rose*, the second example, is hollow-handled with a stainless blade marking it as about 50 years old. The last example, by Tiffany, does not have a maker's mark but only the letter 'H', which may stand for Heavy gauge sterling. Since the pattern does not show up in sterling pattern books, the assumption can be made that the knife was sold by Tiffany, but made up by one of their suppliers. Many large jewelers bought goods and applied their own names, and at times they left the original manufacturer's mark on the piece. Tiffany did not begin to manufacturer its own sterling flatware until Edward C. Moore was integrated into the firm in 1868. Tiffany's introduced thirteen new sterling patterns from 1868 to 1872, many of which are attributed to Moore.

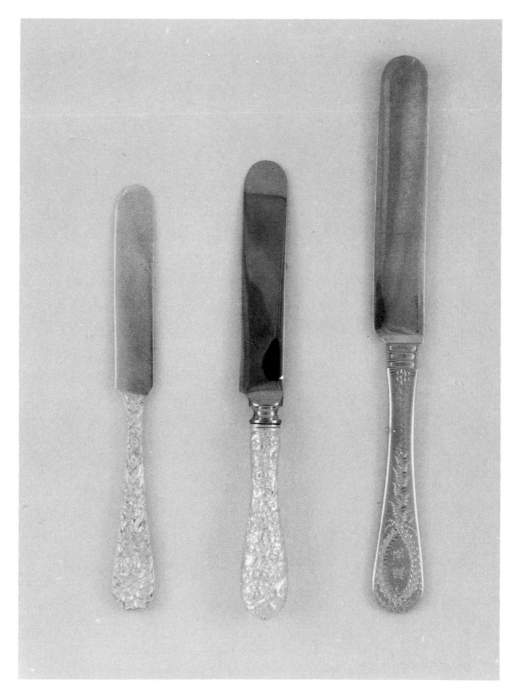

Figure 1.58, Children's Knives: Kirk's *Repoussé* all-silver youth knife, 5 1/2"; Stieff's *Rose*, youth knife, 5 7/8"; and Tiffany's unknown pattern, all-silver youth knife, 7 1/8".

Food Pushers

Figure 1.59 shows four food pushers. Food pushers were designed to assist young children to move their food onto a fork or spoon Food pushers are all individual and unique, and many people have large collections of them.

The two pieces in Gorham's *Strasbourg* (Figure 1.59) are a mid-sized fork and a mid-sized spoon, useful for young children. They are seldom made today, even though they are items that manufacturers could easily produce.

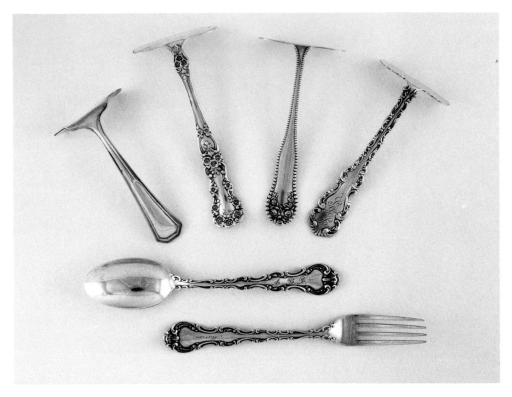

Figure 1.59, Food Pushers and Mid-Size Children's Silver:
Top row, Food Pushers: Lunt's unknown pattern, 3 1/16"; Gorham's *Buttercup*, 4"; *Lancaster*, 3 11/16"; and Whiting's *Louis XV*, 3 11/16".
Bottom row, Mid-Size Children's Silver: Gorham's *Strasbourg*, spoon, 5 1/8", and fork, 5 3/8", sized between baby sets and youth sets.

Figure 1.60 shows a variety of sizes of food-pushers. The smallest one is approximately half the size of the largest. The most unusual pusher is perhaps Alvin's *Bridal Rose*. The part that pushes the food is very unique because of its shape, a gentle curve.

Figure 1.60, Food Pushers: unknown pattern, 2 1/2"; Kirk's *Repoussé*, 3 1/8"; Alvin's *Bridal Rose*, 4 1/16"; and Stieff's *Rose*, 4 1/4".

Youth Sets, Tea Sets, or Breakfast Sets

Figure 1.61 shows a wide variety of patterns and shapes available within this category. Pieces range from plated blade knives, stainless blade knives, to all-silver knives. The forks and spoons are constant—that is, they are all small forks and small spoons.

Figure 1.61, Youth Sets, Tea Knives and Forks, and Breakfast Sets:
Top row: Towle's *King Richard*, knife, 6 1/4", fork, 6 3/8", and spoon, 5 1/2"; Wallace's *Grand Colonial*, knife, 7 1/16", fork, 5 11/16", and spoon, 5 5/16"; Gorham's *Buttercup*, knife, 7 1/2", fork 5 15/16", and spoon, 5 1/2"; Whiting's *Louis XV*, knife, 7 13/32", fork 6 1/8", and spoon, 5 1/4".
Bottom row: Kirk's *Repoussé*, knife, 7 3/16", fork, 6 5/16", and 5 7/16"; Dominick and Haff's *Pointed Antique*, knife, 7 21/32", fork, 6 1/2", and spoon, 5 3/8"; Gorham's *Lancaster*, knife, 7 9/16", fork, 6 29/32", and spoon 5 13/16"; and Reed and Barton's *Francis I*, knife, 7", fork, 5 21/32", and spoon, 5 7/16".

Unusual Place Pieces
Lobster Crackers

A lobster cracker is an unusual and rare scissors like implement for cracking lobster shells, especially claw and tail shells. These utensils are especially useful for Maine lobsters with large claws. (West Coast lobsters do not have the large claws.) Why more manufacturers did not market such a tool for this very popular food is a mystery, as lobsters have been an important part of American cuisine for years. It is nice to be able to add a sterling lobster cracker when using sterling, china, crystal, and good linen. Close examination of the Figure 1.62 reveals the sterling mark and three numbers, but alas, no manufacturer's mark or name.

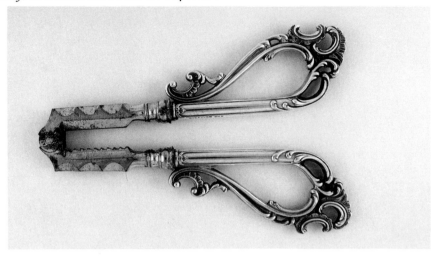

Figure 1.62, Lobster Cracker: Unknown pattern, 5 3/16".

Individual Asparagus Tongs

Individual asparagus tongs are sterling items with a specialized area that is designed to hold one separate spear of asparagus. Some manufacturers have used the almost perpendicular type as represented by Gorham's *Lancaster*, while other manufacturers have adapted Whiting's example, in which the area to hold the asparagus appears to be an extension of the tong handle.

Figure 1.63a, Individual Asparagus Tongs: Whiting's *Louis XV*, 4 1/2"; Gorham's *Lancaster*, 4 1/8", and Whiting's *Louis XV*, 4 1/2".

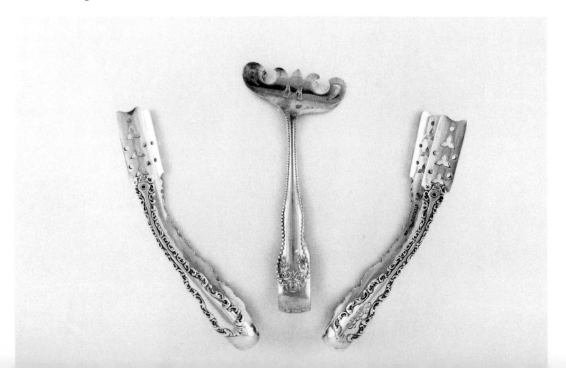

Individual asparagus tongs were made in only a few of the most popular patterns. They are relatively rare items to find. Though interesting, individual asparagus tongs are not practical to use because if the asparagus is over cooked, the juice drips onto the eater's chin. In Figure 1.13b the individual tongs are shown with a Haviland asparagus plate. The plate has indentations for the asparagus and a dipping sauce, be it hollandaise or mayonnaise. The Haviland asparagus plate, shown with Gorham's *Lancaster* individual asparagus tongs and an asparagus serving fork, demonstrates how well the Victorians coordinated sterling flatware and china. They not only designed silver flatware for most food items, but they also created pieces of china as well.

Figure 1.63b, Individual Asparagus Plate and Individual Asparagus Tongs: Haviland's *President Carrot* on a Marseille blank (c. 1880s) and Gorham's *Lancaster*, 4 1/8". Courtesy of David Reichard.

Individual Knife Sharpeners

Individual knife sharpeners are very rare. They were probably used with individual bird knives while eating fowl. Each person would have a sharpener accompanying the individual bird knife. Most likely they would have been placed at the top of the plate and removed after the bird course was completed.

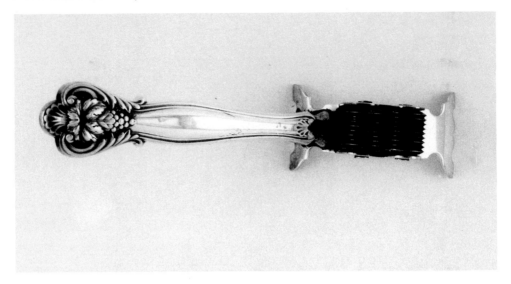

Figure 1.64, **Individual Knife Sharpener:** Durgin's *Vintage*, 5".

Individual Corn Items

Individual corn holders are one of a variety of implements designed for eating corn. Some sets came with matching individual butter pats as well. These particular corn cob holders would be inserted into the end of the ear of corn to assist in holding the hot, buttered corn cob. The holders may have been passed to each diner, or inserted into the cobs before serving.

In Gorham's *Chantilly* sterling pattern a corn fork was made which was similar to the large individual salad/fish fork, but the connecting tines had two sharp cutting points to assist in removing the corn kernels from the corn cobs. These forks were patented in 1911.

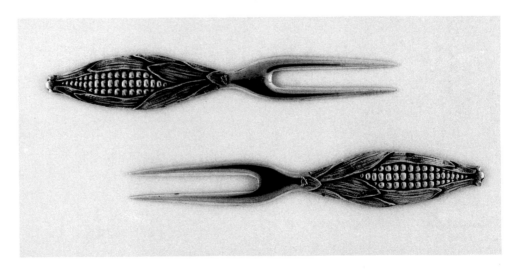

Figure 1.65, **Corn Items:** unknown manufacturer, unknown pattern, 4".

Part 2: Place Settings

Sterling silver represents the ultimate in dining elegance. Even though silver does not contribute to the taste of food, it enhances the dining experience. Silver represents elegance and fine taste. When silver is used it acquires beauty from use which is called patina. Use, coupled with care, helps create treasured mementos from generation to generation.

Through a lifetime, a collector's tastes change, and those who originally chose plain items later seem to swing to ornate patterns. Few people appear to be happy with their choices over a long period of time. Regardless of what a collector chooses, time and tastes change and a person should realize that they will most likely add dishes, crystal and even silver either by purchase or inheritance.

My advice for novice collectors is to choose a silver flatware pattern and let its style and design dictate what goes with it. Bridal consultants at large department stores can suggest coordinating china and crystal patterns, but remember you will be living with the items for a long time, so trust your own judgment. The best advice for a young couple is to choose a good set of plain white china and then coordinate silver and crystal with it.

Different place mats can change the mood and later, when you can afford to add another set of china, it can easily be coordinated with the silver and crystal. One suggestion would be to contrast designs with china, crystal, and sterling to give the best balance between the areas. Two of the areas could be elaborate and the third plain, or two areas plain and one elaborate. Remember, trust your own judgment.

This section deals with eighteen individual sterling patterns and a variety of the implements that have been produced in these patterns. The photographs do not show all the place pieces in a particular pattern, but only those that the collector of each pattern has assembled. Some of the silver is shown with the china that the owner of the pattern uses, and in some cases only the silver is shown. The discussion includes Durgin's *Dauphin*, Gorham's *Strasbourg, Lancaster, Buttercup, King Edward, Crown Baroque, Old Sovereign* and *La Scala*; Wallace's *Grand Colonial*; Towle's *King Richard*; International's *Prelude*; Reed and Barton's *Francis I, Hepplewhite* and *Marlborough*; Dominick and Haff's *Priscilla*; Kirk-Stieff's *Repoussé* and *Corsage*; and Whiting's *Louis XV*.

Dauphin by DURGIN

Introduced in 1897

Gorham, the successor to Durgin, describes the *Dauphin* pattern this way:

> A rich and intricate design of three clusters of roses adorns the *Dauphin* sterling flatware pattern. The roses floral motif is added in an informal manner to show the spontaneity of design. Originally introduced in 1897, *Dauphin* is a delicate and feminine pattern, and its traditional luxuriousness is suitable for today's table.

The following photographs of the pattern illustrate how the flowers on handles of the individual pieces sometimes flow onto the bowls of several of the pieces. This decoration has a delightful effect. Both the front and the reverse sides of *Dauphin* are decorated. Decorating the reverse of place pieces is the European fashion, and it offers the owner the choice of an American setting (with the place pieces right side up) or the European setting (with the forks and spoons turned upside down to expose the beautiful design).

In an old undated brochure by the Daniel Low Company, a large mail order jeweler in business in the early 1900s, the design was called *La France*. Turner (1971) addresses the problem of different names by stating that the "...large mail-order houses, perhaps in an effort to make it appear that certain patterns were their own exclusive property, frequently applied their own names to standard patterns." All this does is add confusion for the new collector and create detours for the serious collector.

Gorham is again offering this pattern as well as a number of other discontinued patterns in its "Masterpiece Collection." Only the basic six-piece place setting and a few serving pieces are currently available. In the following photographs the reader will see presented a collection of *Dauphin* that has been collected over a period of twenty years. The photos show individual forks, knives and spoons, and a complete place setting with china, crystal, and linen plus a dessert setting.

Figure 2.1:
Knives: Dinner knife (blunt), 9 5/8"; dinner knife (French), 9 1/2"; luncheon/dessert knife (French), 8 5/8"; all-silver fish knife, 7 3/4"; and small butter knife, 5 5/16."
Forks: Dinner fork, 7 5/8"; fish fork, 7 1/8"; luncheon or dessert fork, 7"; salad fork, 6 1/4"; pastry fork, 6 1/8"; ice cream fork, 5 7/8"; terrapin fork, 5 1/4"; cocktail fork, 5 1/2"; and strawberry fork, 4 3/4".
Spoons: Dessert spoon, 7 1/8"; bouillon spoon, 5 11/16"; citrus spoon, 5 13/16"; ice cream spoon, 5 3/4"; teaspoon, 5 3/4"; long-handled chocolate spoon, 5 1/2"; tipped chocolate spoon, 4 1/4"; round bowl chocolate spoon, 4 1/4"; and demitasse spoon, 4 3/16".

Figure 2.2: A dinner party set, with Durgin's *Dauphin* silver, Wedgwood's *Mimosa* china, and Ragaska crystal from Yugoslavia.

Figure 2.3: The dessert course, using a Cobalt German Rhine wine, an American cut class ice cream dish, a *Dauphin* ice cream spoon, a demitasse spoon, and a demitasse cup and saucer in the *Mimosa* pattern. *Dauphin* is truly a beautiful floral sterling pattern that blends well with some floral china, but works particularly well with plain china patterns. The *Mimosa* china harmonizes with the array of flowers on the sterling flatware. The platinum edge on the china coordinates the sterling and china.

$\mathscr{S}$trasbourg by GORHAM

Introduced in 1897

The design patent for *Strasbourg* is dated November 16, 1897, but was filed on October 6, 1897 by the Gorham Company of Providence, Rhode Island. The exact designer of *Strasbourg*, according to Melissa McKee, Marketing Services Coordinator for Gorham, cannot be specifically named. The copyrighted records name the design director, but this is not necessarily the individual who created the exact design. Gorham supplied the following description for the pattern:

> A gay informal pattern from the luxurious period of Louis XV inspired by the Rococo design of light-hearted scrolls with an occasional shell for balance. Its decorative scrolls increase with size to the top of the handle, and extend into bowls and tines, collect light and impart an unusual luster.

Strasbourg has been produced for almost a hundred years and through this time Gorham has produced many sterling place and serving items, as well as silver-plated hollow-ware items ranging from serving dishes and chafing dishes to tea sets. In addition, many unusual sterling serving items were made in *Strasbourg* and can be located in Antique shows, estate sales, and sterling matching services through diligent searching. These items include jam spoons, butter pick forks, and tea strainers. In this section the place pieces are compared to a master list of items in a 1911 catalog of *Strasbourg*.

Figure 2.4, Gorham's *Strasbourg*:
Forks: Dinner fork, 7 7/8"; place fork, 7 5/8"; luncheon fork, 7"; individual salad fork, large or individual fish fork, large, 6 7/8"; salad fork, 6 3/8"; individual salad fork, small or individual fish fork, small, 5 7/8"; ice cream fork, large, 5 3/4"; cocktail fork, 5 1/2"; terrapin fork, 5 1/32"; ice cream fork, small, 4 15/16"; and strawberry fork, 4 5/8".
Knives: Dinner knife (French), 9 1/2"; place knife (modern), 9 1/4"; luncheon knife (French), 9"; fish knife, all-silver tea knife or dessert knife, fruit knife, 6 5/8"; butter spreader, hollow-handled, 6 1/4"; all-silver butter spreader, flat, 6".
Spoons: Iced tea spoon, 7 5/8"; dessert spoon, 7 1/8"; cream soup spoon, 6 1/8"; teaspoon, 5 15/16"; ice cream spoon, 5 1/4"; bouillon spoon, 5 1/8"; demitasse spoon, 5 1/8", and salt spoon, 2 13/16".

Figure 2.5: The three types of soup spoons—the bouillon spoon, the cream soup spoon, and the formal soup or dessert spoon—are shown with the accompanying china items—the bouillon cup and underplate, the cream soup and stand, and the rim formal soup. At a formal table the dessert spoon would be correct to use with the rim soup bowl, but a large round bowl soup spoon is used for informal gatherings or for family dinners, paired with a 'coupe' soup plate (a soup plate without a rimmed edge).

In a complete formal dinner setting the following china and silver are used for each course. Five photographs featuring Lenox's *Tuxedo* china illustration the progression of courses.

Figure 2.6: The appetizer course, with a cocktail glass and a cocktail fork. To begin the dinner, a cold appetizer is served.

Figure 2.7: The next course is the fish course, served on the luncheon plate. After this course the fish plate and the service plate are removed.

Figure 2.8: The next course is the main course, served on the dinner plate.

Figure 2.9: The next course would be the salad, just before dessert. An alternative is to serve the salad first, soup second, the fish, and then the entree. The order of the courses is all a matter of preference, and depends on available china and crystal.

Figure 2.10: The last course is dessert, which may be served in a matching rimmed sauce dish on top of a luncheon plate. Coffee and dessert wine may be served at this time, too. All of this, sans food, can be seen in the preceding illustrations, featuring Lenox's *Tuxedo*.

Service plates were very popular earlier this century and they are currently being produced by a number of china manufacturers. A service plate remains at each place on the table until after the soup course or at most through two courses. Then it is replaced with the dinner plate and the rest of the meal continues. Service plates can be made of anything from sterling to china, glass or even wood. Service plates should be chosen to coordinate with the china, crystal, and silver to be used. In an informal setting, a wooden service plate could be best used as a place mat.

There are many glasses made in some services and, just as in silver services, each has a special job. Collectors need to know what each one is designed to be used for; then they should feel free to change the rules to fit their collection.

Figure 2.11: The glassware pictured here is *Regent* by Stuart, which was discontinued in the late 1980s. Each of the glasses has a specific job, but that can be altered to suit the occasion. The glasses, in descending order, are: goblet, flute champagne, saucer champagne, small size wine (this was the only size available when the set was purchased, but later two different sizes were added), port, cocktail, sherry, and cordial glass. In addition the collector has available Blue and Cranberry Hock wines that are used with special dessert wines or to give color to the setting or even to coordinate with the floral and/or linen arrangements.

To illustrate the variety of glassware available, a 1991 catalog of Waterford's *Lismore* pattern lists the following glasses in production:

Tall Stem Hock	Old Fashioned, 9 oz.
Liquor/Cordial	Double Old Fashioned,
Port	12 oz.
Sherry	Tumbler, 10 oz.
White Wine	Highball, 12 oz.
Red Wine (Claret)	Iced Tea
Goblet	Grapefruit

Tall Continental	Footed Dessert
Champagne	Variety Dessert Bowl
Saucer Champagne	Pitcher, 1 1/2 pints
Brandy Snifter	Oversized Wine
Tumbler, 5 oz.	Decanter

This list shows the great number and variety of glass products that are still available.

Storage can eventually become a problem with all these items, so collectors should carefully choose only those items they know they will use.

Lancaster by GORHAM

Introduced in 1897

Gorham's pattern *Lancaster* is truly representative of the late Victorian times. An old ad supplied the following description from the Gorham Company in describing the pattern *Lancaster:*

An elegant, classic styling appropriate for informal or formal settings. Beading and a floral-tipped handle describe the pattern... The designer in this case has introduced the rose and bead pattern giving it a very modern appearance.

Figure 2.12, Gorham's *Lancaster:*
Forks: Dinner fork, 7 5/8"; pie fork, large, 7"; salad fork, large or individual fish fork, large, 7"; luncheon or dessert fork, 7"; ice cream fork, large, 5 3/4"; salad fork, small, or individual fish fork, small, 5 1/2"; cocktail fork, 5 1/2"; individual ice cream fork, small, 5 1/16"; ramekin fork, 5"; and strawberry or berry fork, 4 9/16".
Spoons: Iced tea spoon, 7 1/2"; dessert spoon, 7"; round bowl soup, 6 3/4"; teaspoon, 5 13/16"; grapefruit, 5 3/4" (note the lip on this piece, slightly larger than the that on the orange spoon); orange spoon, 5 11/16"; ice cream spoon, large, 5 3/8"; five o'clock teaspoon, 5 5/16"; bouillon spoon, 5 1/8"; egg spoon, 5"; long-handled chocolate spoon, 4 3/4"; chocolate spoon, small, 4 1/16"; demitasse spoon, 3 7/8"; and individual salt spoon, 2 11/16". To the right of the knives, an individual asparagus tongs, 4 1/8", is shown.
Knives: Dinner knife, large (blunt bladed), 9 9/16"; luncheon or dessert knife (silver-plated blunt nickel steel blade), 9 1/8"; luncheon or dessert knife (blunt bladed), 8 1/2"; tea knife, (plated blade), 7 9/16"; orange knife, 7 3/8"; fruit knife, 6 3/4'; butter spreader modern blade, 6 1/4"; and flat spreader, 5 7/8".

Figure 2.13: Haviland's *Ransom* is set for the first course of a dinner with a ramekin cup and a ramekin fork. The second course would be a salad, and then the entree served on the dinner plate. The dessert silver is at hand, teaming the bird fork and the fruit knife for fruit and cheese. Tea or coffee could be served either with or after dinner.

Figure 2.14: The *Lancaster* place setting is used with a Haviland Well and Tree plate, a very rare item. Note that the dinner-size knife and fork are used with the large individual salad fork. *Photograph by David Reichard*

Buttercup by GORHAM

Introduced in 1899

Occasionally a piece of Gorham's *Buttercup pattern* will be found with the 1900 date, but 1899 was the introduction date of this sterling design. A description of the pattern comes from Gorham and incorporates a description from its 1910-1911 catalog:

> An everlasting bouquet of delicate flowers intricately wrought in silver describes the pattern *Buttercup*. The beautiful and familiar buttercup has been used as the principal decorative motif, avoiding in its treatment all crudity yet retaining the conventional in flower and foliage. In the handle every detail is brought out in strong relief. In the decoration of the bowls and tines of the fancy pieces the designer has been most successful in producing an effect in harmony with the general design.

Figure 2.15, Gorham's *Buttercup*:
Forks: Strawberry fork, 4 9/16"; cocktail fork, 5 1/2"; tea fork, 5 15/16"; salad fork, 6 5/8"; luncheon fork, 7"; place fork, 7 1/2".
Knives: Place knife, 9 1/16"; luncheon knife, 8 3/4"; tea knife, 7 1/2"; fruit knife, 6 7/8"; hollow-handled butter spreader, 6 1/4".
Spoons: Cream soup spoon, 6 1/4"; teaspoon, 5 3/4"; five o'clock spoon, 5 7/16"; youth spoon, 5 1/2"; egg spoon, 5"; demitasse spoon, 4 1/8".

Figure 2.16: Charming English earthenware in the *Calico* pattern harmonizes with Gorham's *Buttercup*. The crystal glass by Mikasa, a sterling pepper by Black, Star, and Frost, an early piece of Sandwich glass, and Whiting's *Lily* master salt help round out the setting. At the top of the dinner plate, a strawberry fork waits to be used with dessert, fresh strawberries.

King Edward GORHAM

Introduced in 1936

A very lovely pattern is Gorham's *King Edward.* The Gorham company describes it as "a traditional elegant Chippendale design," saying that "the pattern features intimate detailing with unusual boldness and depth."

Figure 2.17:
Forks: Lemon fork, 4 3/8"; strawberry fork, 4 11/16"; cocktail fork, 5 3/8"; salad fork, 6 3/8"; luncheon fork, 7 1/8"; dinner fork, 7 11/16".
Knives: Dinner knife, 9 1/2"; steak knife, 9 3/16"; luncheon knife, 8 15/16"; hollow-handled butter spreader, 6 3/16"; flat butter spreaders, 5 13/16".
Spoons: Iced tea spoon, 7 1/2"; dessert spoon, 6 7/8"; place spoon, 6 3/4"; cream soup spoon, 6 1/4"; bouillon spoon, 5 9/16"; teaspoon, 5 15/16"; demitasse spoon, 4 5/32"; and salt spoon, 2 13/16".

Figure 2.18: This place setting rests on a handmade lace placemat. Gorham's *King Edward* is used with gold-banded Minton china and New Martensville Crystal. An American cut glass ice cream dish is used for a shrimp appetizer. A Beleek salt with the Gorham sterling spoon, and flowers in a cobalt blue Polish vase harmonize to make this a truly elegant setting.

Crown Baroque by GORHAM

Introduced in 1975

This very ornate sterling pattern was probably produced as another example designed to compete with the ornate patterns of other manufacturers. Gorham describes *Crown Baroque* as:

Luxurious **weight** and magnificent detail on both the front and back of each piece describes *Crown Baroque*. Each line and decorative motif gracefully creates a harmonious movement of elegant detail. Beautifully balanced and proportioned, the intricate detail is painstakingly executed.

Figure 2.19, Gorham's *Crown Baroque:* Included here are a lemon fork, 4 3/8"; cocktail fork, 5 1/16'; salad fork, 6 3/4"; dinner fork, 7 15/16"; dinner knife, 9 7/8"; steak knife, 9 3/4"; butter knife, 6 1/2"; iced tea spoon, 7 9/16"; place spoon, 6 7/16"; teaspoon, 6 1/8"; and demitasse spoon, 4 7/16".

La Scala by GORHAM

Introduced in 1965

Gorham's *La Scala* pattern was designed by Peter C. Gavette. Gorham furnished the following description of the pattern:

> *La Scala* is a rich, pierced Baroque design. Intricate detail is painstakingly executed. Roses and flowers intertwine with rich scrolls and intricate bead work along the handles.

Figure 2.20: The basic six-piece place setting of Gorham's *La Scala* is shown here, including a salad fork, 6 3/8"; place fork, 7 1/2"; hollow-handled butter spreader, 6 1/2"; place knife (modern), 9"; teaspoon, 6 1/4"; place spoon, 6 5/8". The accompanying china is mixed. The floral pieces are *Old Ivory*, a pattern from Silesia, and the plain pieces are Royal Daulton's *Old Lace*. The relish dish to the left of the plate can hold iced vegetables, and the small vase is actually a toothpick holder in Old Ivory. To the right of the flowers is a cut glass butter pat. The salad plate, along with the butter knife, rests upon Royal Doulton's *Old Lace*. The delicate gold border on the dinner plate coordinates with the gold border on the salad plate. The crystal is Mikasa. The roses in the china compliment the roses on the sterling. The small cut glass butter pat holds just enough butter for one serving.

Grand Colonial by WALLACE

Introduced in 1942

This pattern was designed by William S. Warren. Wallace describes the pattern as having a three-dimensional design, and a brochure illustrating Wallace patterns discusses it, saying that

Unassuming elegance was the hallmark of American style in the colonial days. The stem of this pattern is sculptured in a shape reminiscent of the fiddle, in lines of unadorned integrity, crowned by a petal scroll tip. The pure simplicity of *Grand Colonial* displays the lustrous properties of sterling silver to the fullest, while providing an ideal background for your personal monogram.

Figure 2.21, Wallace's *Grand Colonial:* Strawberry fork, 5"; cocktail fork, 5 9/16"; tea, breakfast or youth fork, 5 11/16"; salad fork, 6 7/16"; place fork (luncheon size), 7 1/4"; place knife (luncheon size, modern), 8 3/4"; tea, breakfast or youth knife (modern), 7 1/16"; hollow-handled spreader, 6 3/16"; flat butter spreader, 6 1/32"; iced tea spoon, 7 1/2"; dessert spoon, 6 15/16"; cream soup spoon, 6"; teaspoon, 6"; grapefruit spoon, 5 7/16"; five o'clock spoon, 5 5/16"; demitasse spoon, 4 1/16"; and salt spoon, individual, 2 3/8."

Figure 2.22: A setting using Lipper's *Blue Danube*, a crystal iced tea glass by Rogaska, and Wallace's *Grand Colonial*, ready for a dinner that begins with French onion soup served in individual covered casseroles. Above the setting, two cut glass salts rest on a small sterling tray with two individual *Grand Colonial* salt spoons. A mug awaits after-dinner coffee. The butter spreader is placed on the butter plate. The napkin has a blue edge that coordinates with the placemat and the blue in the china.

Figure 2.23: This table setting can be used for a Chinese dinner, with only a luncheon fork and teaspoon in Gorham's *Chantilly* necessary. The food is placed on the small platter, rice goes in the rice bowl on the left, and dipping sauces in the open salt and pepper dish. A cut glass drinking glass is included for water and handleless cup is placed on the right for Chinese tea.

King Richard by TOWLE

Introduced in 1932

Brochures distributed by Towle describe *King Richard* in the following manner:

King Richard has a regal dignity and restraint that sets it apart from all other richly decorated patterns. The stateliness of the pointed oval top framed in curling leaves, the rich ornamental shield set below the initial space, the depth ornamentation, all make *King Richard* unmatched by any other pattern.

Figure 2.24: The *King Richard* pattern:

Knives: Dinner knife, 9 1/2"; luncheon knife, 8 5/8"; fish knife, hollow-handle, 8 3/8"; steak knife, 8 3/8"; buffet knife (youth knife or tea knife), 6 1/4"; hollow-handle spreader with sterling blade, 5 11/16".

Forks: Dinner fork, 7 7/8"; luncheon fork, 7 3/8"; fish fork, hollow-handled, 7 3/8"; salad fork, 6 9/32"; youth fork or tea fork 6 3/16"; cocktail fork, 5 27/32"; ice cream fork, 5 5/8"; lemon fork, 5"; and strawberry fork, 4 7/8".

Spoons: Iced tea spoon, 8 3/16"; dessert spoon, 7 1/4"; cream soup spoon, 6 1/16"; grapefruit spoon, 5 7/8"; teaspoon, 6"; bouillon spoon, 5 7/16"; five o'clock teaspoon, 5 1/2"; and demitasse spoon, 4 1/2".

Figure 2.25: This setting features Towle's *King Richard*. A Lenox dinner plate with a green mark is shown with the backstamp "Silver Lenox 1830/2 93.B Q." The vibrant cobalt blue border is highlighted by the intricate silver overlay work. A Stieff *Rose* sterling butter plate and crystal of unknown origins complete this setting.

$\mathcal{P}$relude by INTERNATIONAL

Introduced in 1939

Prelude, designed by Alfred G. Kintz, has been a remarkable line for International, repeatedly one of the most popular patterns. The flowers appear at the base of the handles, and the handle is smooth with a capping of flowers and leaves at the end of the handles. *Prelude* appears to coordinate well with many different kinds of china and crystal. The designer, Alfred G. Kintz, worked at International for forty-five years, from 1910 until his retirement in 1959, with time out for war work. His masterpiece was described in the following manner:

Slender and graceful, *Prelude* contrasts deep-carved floral ornaments with smooth, simple lines to create a refined pattern that is always in good taste, correct with any style, any table setting. Raised borders along the fluted stem enhance the sophisticated simplicity and understated elegance of this ageless design, which remains a favorite.

Figure 2.26: International's *Prelude* is teamed with Mikasa's *Old Lace*, a cobalt blue Rhine Wine glass and a cobalt tumbler, and is set on some exquisite handmade lace. The monogrammed linen is an excellent example of delicately colored damask. The warm ivory and gold tones of the china blend very well with the linen. The cobalt blue glasses enhance the entire setting.

Francis I by REED and BARTON

Introduced in 1906

Francis I is truly one of the outstanding sterling patterns of the twentieth century because of the fifteen design variations found on the handles. Reed and Barton supplied the following information regarding the pattern:

Around 1904-1906, Reed and Barton sought to develop a sterling flatware pattern that would be a marvel of design and craftsmanship representing magnificence in detail and boldness of ornamental relief. Years of careful planning and accurate craftsmanship were responsible for this masterpiece. The designer was Ernest Mayer, a designer who brought years of experience, and a thorough knowledge of the perfection of his art. The pattern is named for Francis of Angouleme, a handsome, talented, debonair, patron of the arts and literature. He was born in 1494 and died in 1547. Francis became King of France in 1515 upon the death of his uncle, Louis XII. His reign was one of splendor. He combined all his talent and that of France developing all to a dazzling height of glory in art and architecture known as French Renaissance.

Even though only seven place pieces of sterling flatware are shown in Figure 2.27, *Francis I* is one of the few current patterns being made with a large number of place pieces. An old brochure for *Francis I* lists thirty different place pieces offered in the pattern. More recently, Reed and Barton had a program that offered some of their old serving pieces and four place pieces made from the original tools and hand-cut dies, using centuries-old silversmithing techniques. The place pieces that were offered were the following: Ice Cream Spoon, Large, 5 1/2"; Chocolate Spoon, 4 1/2"; Ramekin Fork, 5 1/4"; and Sherbet Spoon, 4 1/2". In the same collection were some fine examples of hollowware in the *Francis I* pattern. Several of the old serving pieces can be found in Part III, Serving Pieces.

Figure 2.27, *Francis I* by Reed and Barton: The following sterling pieces are pictured here: a salad fork, 6 1/8"; luncheon fork, 7 1/8"; dinner fork, 7 27/32"; dinner knife (French blade), 9 5/8"; luncheon knife, 8 13/16", teaspoon, 5 13/16" (used with the bouillon cup). The china is *Indian Tree*, a pattern made by Coalport from 1801 until about the mid-1980s. The tumbler and the Hock wine glass are both cranberry and coordinate with the colors in the china. Coalport designed the pattern to help meet the competition for porcelain goods from the Orient. The oriental feel of the design was planned specifically to attract business back to English china. Ships of the time carried imported Chinese porcelain below the water line for ballast, as the water did not damage it. This pattern has the coloring of an export pattern, "Rose Medallion."

ℋepplewhite by REED and BARTON

Introduced in 1907

An old undated brochure from Reed and Barton describes the *Hepplewhite* pattern as the following:

> The noted English designer and cabinet-maker [Hepplewhite] produced some of the finest work of the eighteenth century. As he himself said, he tried "to unite elegance and utility." He attained a grace and refinement of the highest type, combined with real simplicity and common sense. The pattern embodies his ideals in their mature perfection. This sterling pattern does just that.

Figure 2.28, *Hepplewhite* by Reed and Barton: the following items are pictured: cocktail fork, 5 7/16"; pie fork, 6"; salad fork, 6"; dinner fork, 7 11/16"; dinner knife, 9 5/8"; all-silver butter spreader, 6 1/32"; large round bowl soup, 7"; iced tea spoon, 7"; teaspoon, 5 3/4"; and demitasse spoon, 4 3/8".

Figure 2.29: In the cheerful holiday setting, Spode's *Christmas Tree* china is paired with Reed and Barton's *Hepplewhite* silver for a truly memorable Christmas meal. A small, round, fluted dish is used for soup. Next, a salad would be served on a square salad plate. The entree would then be served on the dinner plate. At the top of the setting, a butter dish and butter spreader have an individual butter pat that could hold flavored butter to complement the meal. Individual salts and peppers, a mug for coffee or tea, and a red glass for water also complement the setting. The monogrammed linen is teamed with a napkin ring monogrammed for the family member to be seated at this particular place.

Marlborough by REED and BARTON

Introduced in 1906

Reed and Barton supplied the following information regarding the *Marlborough* pattern;

No silver pattern of today exemplifies so well the best of Victorian design as does Reed and Barton's *Marlborough* for here is a pattern that speaks of the mid-Victorian era. Then, design was formal but not fussy, elegant but not pompous. *Marlborough's* graceful curves and scrolls, set off by the gleam of the center panel, recaptures the grandeur and romance of English court tradition. Yet, *Marlborough* is a contemporary sterling, as fit for a bride's first supper as for a diplomat's state dinner.

Figure 2.30: The following pieces are all in the *Marlborough* pattern: salad fork, 6 1/16"; luncheon fork, 7 3/16"; dinner fork, 7 3/4"; dinner knife, 9 5/8"; luncheon knife (stainless steel), 9 1/8"; luncheon knife (modern), 8 7/8"; hollow-handled butter spreader (modern), 6 7/16"; butter spreader hollow-handled, 6 3/16"; flat, paddle-shaped butter spreader, 5 15/16"; iced tea spoon, 7 5/8"; cream soup spoon, 5 3/4"; teaspoon, 5 13/16."

Figure 2.31: This Christmas dining experience features Lenox's *Holiday* china and *Marlborough* sterling. The basic five-piece china set and five pieces of silver are grouped with linen placemats and matching napkins, along with a green-overlay juice glass and a green-stemmed wine glass. The subtle greens in the china and in the glassware help make the red berries intertwined with holly even more rich and festive.

Priscilla by DOMINICK and HAFF

Introduced in 1916

The *Priscilla* pattern by Dominick and Haff is a variation of the popular *Pointed Antique* pattern, which was introduced circa 1895. The pattern was designed by Dominick and Haff, and it in turn became part of Reed and Barton when Reed and Barton purchased the firm in 1928. Reed and Barton supplied the following information about *Pointed Antique*:

No modern day pattern in American history has enjoyed so much popularity over so many years as has Reed and Barton's famous *Pointed Antique*. *Pointed Antique*'s popularity has increased in the last few years. *Pointed Antique* is an authentic reproduction of an original spoon design made by Paul Revere and now on display at the Metropolitan Museum of Art. *Priscilla* is a decorated version of *Pointed Antique*.

Figure 2.32, *Priscilla* by Dominick and Haff: Salad fork, 6 5/16"; luncheon fork, 7 5/32"; dinner fork, 7 15/16"; dinner knife, 9 5/8"; luncheon knife, 8 1/2"; butter spreader, flat, 5 7/8"; large round bowl soup spoon, 7 1/4"; bouillon spoon, 5 3/8"; teaspoon, 5 3/4"; ice cream spoon, 5 9/16".

Repoussé by KIRK-STIEFF

Introduced in 1828

Gorham, the successor to the Kirk-Stieff companies, provided this description of *Repoussé:*

> This overall floral pattern is named for the intricate art of repoussé, [and was] developed by Samuel Kirk in 1820. The pattern design involves the craft of bumping up sections of a hollow piece of metal from the inside, and sculpting the raised area into flowers and foliage designs by hammering. This ornate design became so identified with the region that the highly decorated look has been known as "Baltimore silver" ever since. Today, the *Repoussé* pattern is still considered the standard in its class and remains the company's most popular pattern.

Figure 2.33: *Repoussé* pattern silver is teamed with a beautiful dinner plate backstamped :

Wm. Guérin and Co.
France
L i m o g e s

The plate has two bands of a deep powdered blue, separated by four bands of gold. The small rosebuds between the blue bands are a deep cranberry color, accented with delicate green leaves located in each cartouche. The cup and saucer are by Lenox. The beautiful Continental sterling ramekin is placed on a Stieff 6" sterling bread and butter plate. The linens are rose damask. The cut glass tumbler is signed by Tuttle.

Figure 2.34: The following items are in the *Repoussé* pattern: lemon fork, 4 1/2"; fruit cocktail fork, 5 1/8"; seafood cocktail fork, 5 5/16"; small ice cream fork, 5 7/16"; large ice cream fork, 6"; salad fork, 6 5/8"; place fork, 7 1/4"; place knife (French), 8 7/8"; place knife, 8 15/16"; hollow-handled butter, 6 7/16"; flat butter, 5 3/16"; iced tea spoon, 7 1/2"; muddler spoon, 7 11/16"; large round bowl soup spoon, 7 5/16"; place spoon, 6 7/16"; cream soup, 6 1/8"; large teaspoon, 5 7/8"; teaspoon, 5 3/4"; bouillon spoon, 5 1/8"; demitasse spoon, 4 5/16".

Corsage by KIRK-STIEFF

Introduced in 1935

This beautiful pattern features orchids with other flowers and leaves, and is one of many patterns similar to *Repoussé*. It has been a highly successful pattern for the Stieff Company. Gorham, the successor to Kirk-Stieff, provided the following:

> A graceful design of interwoven leaves and scrolls surrounds this lovely pattern. The profusion of flowers with two orchids at the end of the handles provides a beautiful balance of foliage and flowers.

All the examples of this pattern that appear in this text were purchased by the father of one of the contributors, and when he gave it as a gift to his wife he commented that, "You'll always have an orchid every day when you use our silver." What a thoughtful comment for a very romantic pattern!

Figure 2.35, Kirk-Stieff's *Corsage:*
A place setting, consisting of a lemon fork, 4 3/4"; salad fork, 6 1/8"; luncheon fork, 7 1/16", place fork, 7 1/16"; place knife, 8 15/16"; luncheon knife, 8 7/8"; flat spreader, 6 1/8"; iced tea spoon, 7 7/16"; parfait spoon, 5 7/8"; teaspoon, 5 7/8"; individual salt spoon, 2 13/16".

Old Sovereign by GORHAM

Introduced in 1941

This pattern was introduced under the name *Sovereign* just before the beginning of World War II, and one may speculate that the war effort slowed, if not stopped, the production of the pattern. Its name was changed to *Old Sovereign* when Gorham developed a new pattern it wished to name *Sovereign*. The following is a description of *Old Sovereign*:

Old Sovereign is a Scandinavian-like design. The traditional column provides grace that is supported by a finial with a pineapple-shell design. The gauge of the sterling is heavy and massive. The bowls of the serving pieces are artistically interpreted.

Figure 2.36, *Old Sovereign* **by Gorham:** This place setting features Aynsley's *Cottage Garden* china, and a bowl with a clamshell design on the exterior is used to serve pea soup. Just above the plates in the center is a small crystal pitcher meant to hold sherry for flavoring the soup. Guests may add as much or as little to the soup as they desire. The delicate rose pink color of the crystal blends with the multi-colored Anysley.

Louis XV by WHITING

Introduced in 1891

Gorham, the successor to Whiting, supplied the following information about *Louis XV*:

Luxurious late Renaissance detail joined in a rhythmic formality describes the decorative scrolls adorning the handle's edge. The flowing, graceful lines of *Louis XV* express femininity and romance.

Whiting must have produced this pattern in great abundance since so many examples can be found today. The *Louis XV*

items pictured throughout the book have been assembled in the last twenty-five years, and new items still surface from time to time. Missing from the pictures are knives with hollow handles, as the collector who contributed this set prefers to use pearl-handled knives.

Many of the pieces presented throughout the text have required careful research. Monograms and even names have been clues to sets and to items that were purchased for children.

Figure 2.37, *Louis XV* by Whiting:

Forks: Dinner fork, 7 1/2"; fish fork, large, 7 1/2"; luncheon fork, 6 7/8"; salad fork, large (supplied by Gorham in 1967), 6 13/16"; bird fork, hollow-handled, 6 5/8"; pickle fork, 6 3/8"; salad fork, small, 6 1/8"; junior fork or tea fork, 6 1/8"; small pie fork, 6 1/16"; ice cream fork, large, 5 15/32"; cocktail fork, 5 1/2"; crab, lobster, or shellfish fork (note that this fork is completely flat) 5 1/2"; terrapin fork, 5 3/8"; ramekin fork, 5 1/16"; and strawberry fork, 5 15/32".

Spoons: Tablespoon, or European soup spoon, 8 3/16"; dessert spoon, 6 7/8"; large round bowl soup spoon, 6 3/4"; short-handled iced tea spoon, 6 3/4"; sorbet spoon, 5 7/8"; ice cream spoon, large, 5 13/16"; teaspoon, 5 3/4"; teaspoon, custom-designed (note the pierced and incised design), 5 3/4"; grapefruit spoon, 5 3/8"; five o'clock teaspoon, 5 1/4"; ice cream spoon, small, 5 1/8"; bouillon spoon, 5"; egg spoon, 4 1/32"; demitasse spoon, 4"; salt spoon, individual, 2 1/4".

Knives: Pearl-handled dinner knife, 9 1/2"; all-silver (A. S.) tea knife or junior knife, 7 13/32"; A. S. large fish knife, 7 5/16"; A. S. fish knife, small, 6 9/16"; A. S. small youth knife, 6 1/2"; A. S. butter spreader, large, 5 11/16"; A. S. paté spreader, 5 3/8"; and A. S. butter spreader, small, 5.' To the right of the knives a pair of asparagus tongs, 4 1/2", is shown.

Figure 2.38: A damask linen napkin is used here as a place mat, and a second matching damask napkin is held by Gorham's *Strasbourg* napkin ring. A service plate in cobalt blue accents the white Wedgwood *Countryware* dishes. The crystal is from Williamsburg and consists of an iced tea glass and a water tumbler. Coffee and iced beverages will be served with the meal and, therefore, an iced tea spoon and a teaspoon are placed on the outside, while the round bowl soup spoon is next to the knife. The meal consists of a cream soup followed by fresh asparagus, which will be served onto the luncheon plate directly underneath the cream soup. Individual asparagus tongs are placed at the top of the setting. The salad fork is included for those who prefer to use it instead of the individual asparagus tongs. The entree would be served on the dinner plate. A bread and butter plate and knife round out this setting. The blue lapis plum adds color, and the mug lends an air of informality, even though the setting could be considered formal.

Figure 2.39: This delightful setting uses three sterling patterns to start the morning: Whiting's *Louis XV* fork, all-silver knife, and spoon, Gorham's *Buttercup* egg spoon, and *Strasbourg's* jam spoon. The china, Wedgwood's *Countryware,* is set for breakfast. The covered dish contains hotcakes, and the egg cup holds an egg cooked to the desire of the guest; there is jam in the shell dish and toast in the toast rack. An individual tea pot, individual sugar and individual cream pitcher round out the setting.

Part 3: Serving Pieces

Introduction

This section deals with serving pieces that were produced by American silversmiths from about the close of the Civil War to the present day. A far smaller number of serving pieces were produced than individual place pieces. Because fewer serving pieces were produced, fewer of these items are available to be found today. Some serving items were produced for only a limited time, and they are even more difficult to locate for that reason. A more recent event may have contributed to the shortage. The high price of silver during the 1980s may have caused much old silver to be melted down.

Most all serving pieces can be grouped into six major categories: Forks, Knives, Spoons, Ladles, Tongs, and Servers and Scoops. There are two additional minor categories: New Hollow-Handled Servers and a group labeled Miscellaneous. The currently produced hollow-handled servers, with different stainless inserts called 'findings' placed into sterling handles, are New Hollow-Handled Servers. All silver manufacturers currently have some of these forms available. The Miscellaneous group includes nut crackers and nut picks, bar items, tea items and Made-up Servers. Made-up Servers, which will be discussed later, refer to items specially made in the silver shops of Shreve and Company and Vanderslice and Co., both old firms with ties to silver's historical past. These makers add their own findings to the antique handles of other makers, creating varied pieces for current use.

Forks

Asparagus Forks

Figure 3.1, Asparagus Forks: Gorham's *Strasbourg*, 9"; Whiting's *Louis XV* (Shreve variation), 10"; Kirk's *Repoussé*, 9 3/8"; Durgin's *Dauphin*, 9 11/16"; Gorham's *Buttercup*, 9 1/8".

Figure 3.2, Asparagus Utensils: Gorham's *Lancaster* asparagus fork, 9 1/4"; *Strasbourg* asparagus tongs, 10"; and *Lancaster* hooded asparagus server, 9".

Many types of utensils have been made to serve asparagus, including asparagus forks, asparagus tongs, and hooded asparagus servers. Two of these three examples in Gorham's *Lancaster* are shown with the *Strasbourg* tongs in Figure 3.2. Silversmiths have even made individual asparagus tongs (See Figure 3.103a). Turner, in his book *American Silver Flatware* (1971), noted that silver manufacturers in the United States introduced the hooded asparagus server and individual asparagus tongs. Asparagus serving tongs were a European invention, and one of the first for American silver manufacturers to reproduce (See Asparagus Tongs, Figure 3.75). Each of the asparagus implements has its advantages, but the hooded asparagus server appears to be the most useful and perhaps the easiest to use. The flat portion lifts the stalks and the rolled hooded end prevents the asparagus from rolling off.

Many of the large asparagus forks have one or more connecting bars near the base of the tines for stability. Forks with the connecting bars in Figure 3.1 include Gorham's *Strasbourg*, Whiting's *Louis XV*, and Durgin's *Dauphin*.

The large Coalport/Wedgwood dish in the *Countryware* pattern shown in the picture is actually a bread basket, but with the Durgin *Dauphin* asparagus fork, the two work superbly well for serving asparagus.

Figure 3.3: Durgin's *Dauphin* asparagus server, 9 11/16", with Wedgwood's *Countryware* bread basket.

In the *Chantilly* pattern by Gorham, two large forks frequently turn up that have been identified as either Asparagus or Toast Forks. This explains why *Chantilly* asparagus forks can have two different types of tines. One is a heavily pierced fork (Figure 3.4) while the other is a wide three-tined fork with delicate piercing between the tines, similar to the *Strasbourg* fork (Figure 3.1). These forks are excellent for asparagus, and those that have flat tines are also good for serving quiche. Gorham's *Buttercup* also came in the two different styles. The 1910-1911 Gorham catalog does not show the example in Figure 3.1, but only a fork labeled as an Asparagus or Toast Fork. An undated copy from an old Gorham catalog featuring *Buttercup* shows the example in Figure 3.1.

In addition to the large asparagus serving forks, many silver companies made beautiful serving trays or dishes for asparagus. Some of the Shreve examples had an area for the asparagus, with two built-in areas for the small sauce boats and ladles they included, one for hollandaise and the other for mayonnaise. Other examples from Tiffany had a sterling tray and an underdish that fitted onto the tray, that was pierced and removable, thus allowing excess liquid to drain from the asparagus. Kirk made its asparagus trays in two parts—a tray and a liner—but marketed the same tray without the liner as an ice cream serving tray. Stieff also made a two-piece tray, but called the pierced liner a "drainer." Any of these items may be available at auctions or found at the larger antique shows.

Bacon Forks

These long handled forks, some with short tines, are not found in all patterns. Usually they are made by Stieff or Kirk. Old Kirk catalogs, circa 1911, list bacon tongs in some patterns, but not all. A 1930s Kirk catalog lists this same fork as a sardine fork, long handled. This is one example of renaming the function of a particular serving piece. Kirk's example has distinct tines, while Stieff's example with the pierced design represents the bacon forks produced by these companies many years ago. For many years the Stieff *Corsage* fork was used at the holiday table to serve small pieces of fruitcake. Today these forks are excellent for serving Dolma or stuffed mushroom caps.

Figure 3.5, Bacon Forks: Stieff's *Corsage*, 8 1/4"; Kirk's *Repoussé*, 7 19/32".

Figure 3.4: Gorham's *Chantilly* asparagus or toast fork, 8 1/2".

Baked Potato Forks

Baked Potato/Sandwich Forks are interesting serving pieces made at the factory from luncheon forks. Two styles are made: in one style the inside two tines are removed and in the other style the outside two tines are removed. A Gorham catalog from the turn of the century featuring *Chantilly* shows a two-tined potato serving fork. A later catalog from 1911 lists it as a baked potato/sandwich fork. The fork in *Plymouth* shows yet another example by Gorham. Brochures by other manufacturers show baked potato/sandwich forks made by companies other than Gorham. The *Imperial Queen* fork by Whiting is an excellent example of the second type of fork—one with the outside tines removed and the inside tines spread out, thus creating a rounded look at the top of what obviously was the tine area.

Currently these forks are being made by some silver dealers from luncheon, place or dinner forks and called English meat forks (with the outside tines turned out and twisted and the center tines removed) or baked potato forks (with the tines turned out but not twisted, and also with the extra tines removed). The decision to add one of these "made up" items to a collection depends on the collector.

Kirk labeled its relish fork as a 'Relish/Baked Potato Fork'. This is another example of how different labels may be applied to a particular piece of silver. The section on Relish Forks, Figure 3.26 includes a picture of this type of fork.

The baked potato/sandwich fork is especially useful for serving potatoes, whether baked, whole, or even sliced. Some open faced sandwiches can be more easily served with a flat server, some waffle knives, or a small tomato or a cucumber server.

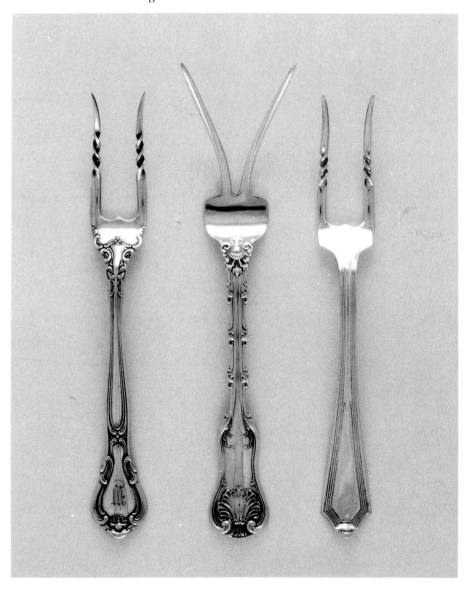

Figure 3.6, Baked Potato or Sandwich Forks: Gorham's *Chantilly*, 7"; Whiting's *Imperial Queen*, 7 7/16"; Gorham's *Plymouth*, 7".

Beef Forks

It is interesting to note how the tines on all the beef forks flare out. This is one distinguishing feature, but not all flared forks are beef forks (See Relish Forks by Kirk Figure 3.26). The flared tines aid in piercing a portion of meat and serving it. Beef forks were introduced to serve already sliced beef. In some patterns there were two sizes. If so, the larger fork is found more frequently, and the small fork is the additional fork. If only one fork was made in a pattern, it is usually the large fork. One exception to this is the example in Whiting's *Louis XV*, where three samples are shown (Figure 3.7 and Figure 3.90). Two samples are from Whiting, and the third sample is from George Shreve and Company. For additional information on made-up servers, see Figures 3.89 and 3.90).

The *Dauphin* beef fork makes an excellent cold meat fork due to its large size. The large fork in *Old French* works equally as well as a bacon serving fork. Any of these forks can easily be used at a large buffet table to serve cheese, cold cuts, and even vegetables such as tomatoes, sliced onions, and lettuce, while preparing sandwiches.

In an undated Gorham catalog featuring *Imperial Chrysan-*

themum, the fork in the photograph is listed as a 'Smoked Beef Fork', yet in another catalog of 1899 featuring *Lancaster*, the same fork is labeled as a 'Beef Fork'. This is another example of varying the name and silver function of a serving piece within a company. Almost all companies are guilty of this game. Some of the misnamings should be blamed on the selling dealer, most likely a jeweler, who through mail-order sale catalogs sold a tremendous amount of sterling flatware. Some mail-order companies even took the liberty of giving different names to well-known patterns, thus adding an additional problem for all but the most serious collector.

Many of the forks came in pairs, as evidenced by Gorham's *Lancaster* and *Strasbourg* (shown in their large and small versions), and Whiting's *Louis XV*. The Durgin fork also came in a small size. The example of *Francis I*'s small beef fork shows another pattern's version. Note how the tines emerge from the large, beautifully pierced area above the tines. The various forms of cold meat forks in Figures 3.16 and 3.17 show the differences in the size and shape of these distinctly different forks.

Figure 3.7, Beef Forks:
Top row: Kirk's *Mayflower*, 6 1/8"; Reed and Barton's *Francis I*, 6 1/8"; Gorham's *Old French*, 7 1/8"; Durgin's *Dauphin*, 7 1/2"; Gorham's *Buttercup*, 6 7/8"; Towle's *Canterbury*, 6 5/16"; and Jenkins and Jenkins, 6 9/16".
Bottom row: Gorham's *Imperial Chrysanthemum*, 6 13/16"; Whiting's *Louis XV*, 5 3/4" and 6 3/4"; Gorham's *Strasbourg*, 6 13/16" and 5 3/4; *Lancaster*, 6 13/16" and 5 3/4".

Butter Picks, Butter Pick-Forks, & Butter Pick-Knives

Butter picks are frequently found and easily identified. Butter picks with twisted stems are used to pick up pats of butter or balls of butter from serving dishes filled with ice. The variations in this utensil occur in the twisted end (Figure 3.9). It is amazing how each company varied its designs to make their implements unique. These variations are very evident in the picture. Durgin's *Dauphin* and Kirk's *Repoussé* are twisted, while Lunt's *Chippendale* and Wallace's *Rose* are very closely twisted. Reed and Barton's *Francis I* is both twisted and pierced. The two examples in Whiting's *Louis XV* vary in length, contributing yet another dimension. Figure 3.09 and Figure 3.10a reveal tremendous

differences between the picks. In Figure 3.09 all of the butter picks are regular with the exception of Reed and Barton's *Francis I*. Looking at the first example in Figure 3.10a by an unknown manufacturer in an unknown pattern, and comparing it to Towle's *Empire*, Schofield's *Mayflower*, and *Baltimore Rose*, the reader can see that each has a thin, long spear-type end, and the example by Kirk in *Repoussé* (third from right) has a most unusual end. It appears to be an almost barb-like instrument. All of these variations contribute to making a collection of butter picks truly unique.

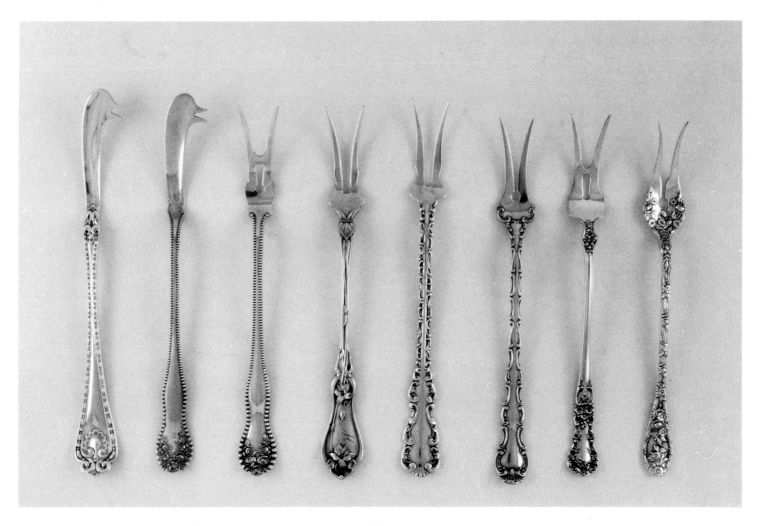

Figure 3.8:
Butter Pick-Knives: Alvin's *Wellington*, 6 3/8"; Gorham's *Lancaster*, 6 1/8";
Butter Pick-Forks: Gorham's *Lancaster*, 5 15/16"; Wallace's *Violet*, 6"; Whiting's *Louis XV*, 6 1/8"; Gorham's *Strasbourg*, 5 15/16"; *Buttercup*, 5 7/8"; and Durgin's *Dauphin*, 5 13/16".

The butter pick-fork performs the same function as a butter pick, that is, to move butter from one dish to another. In Figure 3.09, Gorham's *Lancaster* and *Buttercup* have crosspieces between the tines, but the other examples, Whiting's *Violet* and *Louis XV*, Durgin's *Dauphin* and Gorham's *Strabourg* do not. The non-crossed forks cuold possibly present another problem. Some companies have introduced old butter pick-forks as the currently produced pickle fork. Not all companies did this, but Gorham, among others, did. If your sterling pattern is by Gorham you can quickly tell if you have a butter pick-fork or a pickle fork by looking at the reverse of the fork. If the words "Gorham Sterling" appear, most likely you have a new fork, and it is not a butter pick-fork. If you find the Gorham manufacturer's mark—a Lion, an anchor, and a capital letter 'G'—you most likely have a butter pick-fork. If your fork has three tines, then it is an old pickle fork.

Additional information gleaned from an undated Reed and Barton brochure advertising its *Hepplewhite* pattern shows three different types of butter pick-forks. One is a twisted stem butter pick, another is a pointed flat pick, and the third is a two-tined fork. All this can become confusing even to the most discriminating collector.

The third utensil found in this category, the butter pick-knife, is represented by two examples in Figure 3.8. The first knife, in Alvin's *Wellington*, closely matched the other example in Gorham's Lancaster. Used with cubed butter, the knife has a cutting edge. The opposite side has two prongs. After one slices the butter, the knife is reversed and the butter is pierced with the two tines and brought to the plate. These items are found from time to time, but they are not plentiful.

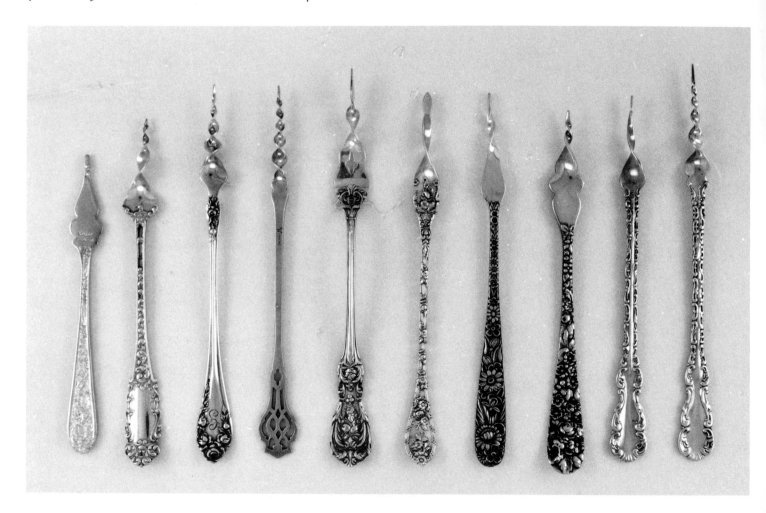

Figure 3.9, Butter Picks: Stieff's *Corsage*, 4 15/16"; Watson, Newell and Company's *Olympia*, 5 11/16"; Wallace's *Rose*, 6 5/32"; Lunt's *Chippendale*, 6"; Reed and Barton's *Francis I*, 6 3/8"; Durgin's *Dauphin*, 6 1/16"; Kirk's *Repoussé*, 6 1/16"; Stieff's *Rose*, 5 7/8"; Whiting's *Louis XV*, 6 7/16" and 6".

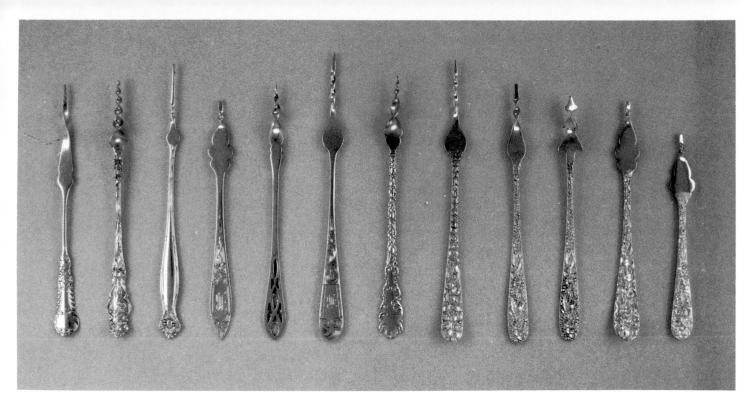

Figure 3.10a: Unknown pattern and manufacturer, 5 7/8"; Wallace's *Irian*, 6"; Towle's *Empire*, 6 7/8"; Stieff's *Lady Claire*, 5 19/32"; unknown pattern and manufacturer, 6"; Schofield's *Mayflower*, 6 3/4"; Wallace's *Waverly*, 6 1/8"; Schofield's *Baltimore Rose*, 6 17/32"; Kirk's *Repoussé*, 6 1/16" and 5 21/32"; Stieff's *Rose*, 5 17/32"; and *Rose*, 4 27/32".

Also pictured in Figure 3.10b with a Haviland butter basket is a *Lancaster* butter pick-knife and a butter pick-fork. The butter pick-knife has a cutting edge and two short tines to pick up a pat of butter after cutting it. The butter pick-fork would be used to serve balls of butter or slices of butter. The Haviland china illustrates the dish manufacturers designed to hold butter balls, butter cubes, or pats of butter served on a bed of ice. The perforation on the top of the dish allows water formed from the melting ice to drain into the dish, so that the butter does not stand in the water.

The section on pickle forks and the section on individual placepieces provides additional information about related flatware.

Figure 3.10b: Pictured with a Haviland butter basket is a *Lancaster* butter pick-knife, with a cutting edge and two short tines on the opposite side to pick up a pat of butter after cutting it. Manufacturers designed dishes like this Haviland china piece to hold butter balls or pats of butter on a bed of ice. The perforation on top of the dish allows the melting ice to drain into the dish.

Cake Forks

Cake forks are rather rare. They usually have long, large tines, some with delicate piercing between the tines, and they are excellent cake serving instruments. Most examples of cake forks were made by Reed and Barton or by Wallace Silversmiths. Whiting's example in *Louis XV* is long and has slender tines. Some companies list the cold meat fork and the cake fork as one and the same. The photograph of the Wallace *Rose* example in Figure 3.11 has a regular handle and a beautifully pierced section between the wide tines. This fork would be useful for cake, but just as easily can be adapted to serving Italian manicotti, or individual portions of jellied salads.

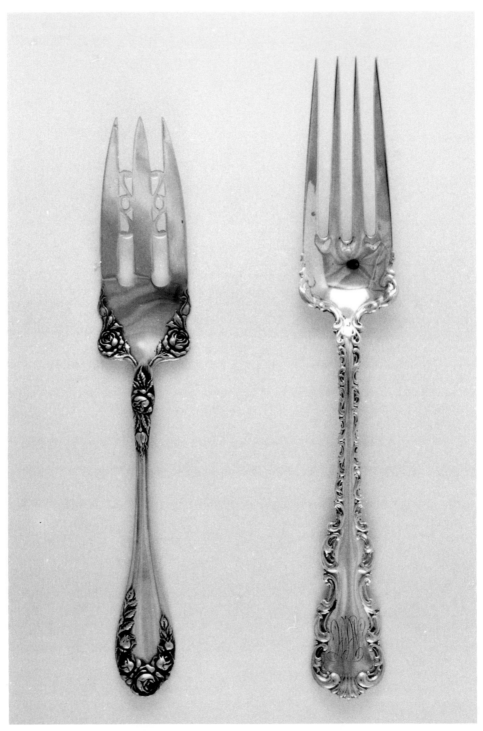

Figure 3.11, Cake Forks: Wallace's *Rose,* 8 1/8"; Whiting's *Louis XV,* 9".

Carving Sets

Carving sets come in three sizes, depending on the manufacturer, and include a carving knife and a carving fork. Other items found in a set might include a carving steel (either long or short to match the size of the set), the carver's assistant (in two sizes), a ham slicer, poultry shears, bone holders (large and individual size for serving squab), and knife sharpeners (large and individual). The carver's assistant is wider than a carving fork and the tines are longer to assist in holding the meat or poultry in place while it is being cut. It can also be used like a fork to serve the meat. Each piece corresponds in size to the other pieces in the set. A carving set used to cut and serve roasted meats has a steel and carver's assistant in the large size, while carving sets for steaks have a steel and carver's assistant in a smaller size. Poultry shears can quickly cut cooked poultry into manageable portions at the table, thus preventing the bird from becoming cold before being served.

Figure 3.12 features Gorham's *Lancaster*, and many of the items made by Gorham for carving sets are shown. The figure has the two sizes of joint holders usually found in Gorham patterns. Next appears the bird set, which is discussed later in this section, and finally the three-piece roast set. The roast set consists of a carving fork with a cutting guard, a steel, and a carving knife. The only missing items are a two-piece steak carving set, and a pair of poultry shears and a bone holder (see Figure 3.14, and note that the individual squab holders are smaller versions of the bone holder) and the small knife sharpener.

Figure 3.12, Carving Forks, Knives, Sets, and Holders: Gorham's *Lancaster* joint holder, small, 8 3/8", and large, 10 7/8; bird fork, 11", and knife, 11 7/8"; roast set, fork, 11 1/8", steel, 14 1/4", and knife, 11 1/8". Not shown is a two-piece steak carving set, which is the smallest set in this pattern.

Figure 3.13 shows the *King Richard* roast carving set by Towle and a ham slicer, and the *Hannah Hull* steak carving set by Tuttle. The large set in *King Richard* makes a statement to assembled guests when the host carves a turkey or standing rib roast. The *Strasbourg* bird set in Figure 3.14 dates from 1897, as evidenced by the Gorham manufacturer's mark found on the two pieces. The manufacturer's mark used by Gorham is an American variation of the English hallmark system. According to Turner (1971), when Gorham began using a maker's mark in 1868 it was made up of a picture of a lion, a picture of an anchor, and the Gothic letter 'G'. Gorham was duplicating the English method of marking silver, but in American fashion. The lion represented silver, the anchor represented Rhode Island (home of the Gorham company), and the 'G' stood for Gorham. The carving set does not have the Gorham name, but only the manufacturer's mark or trademark, the word sterling, and the selling jeweler's mark. In this example, all the items bear the name of Shreve and Company, a San Francisco jeweler who began business in 1852, and is still located on the corner of Powell and Post Streets in San Francisco. The marks represent a guarantee or quality for any American sterling manufacturer.

Old silver produced in Maryland exhibited another system for marking sterling. A Maryland law of 1815 required all Baltimore silver to be stamped with the arms of the city of Baltimore, the date letter and the head of liberty. The mark assured quality somewhere between coin and sterling. By 1830 this whole system was disbanded, partly due to the increased cost it created for silversmiths. Other silver manufacturers had their own marks which were quickly identifiable to the trained eye.

The *Strasbourg* set features old carbon steel fork tines and knife blade, which stain no matter how they are polished, but the blade cuts beautifully. At one time, when game was commonly served as one course at a formal dinner, the bird set and the individual bird knife and individual bird fork were a necessity. These individual pieces were made in the pattern *Chantilly* by Gorham (not shown). They were sterling hollow-handled with blades and tines made of carbon steel. The same individual bird forks and individual bird knives appear on *Strasbourg* lists. An example of Bird Forks can be found in Figure 1.14. An old Reed and Barton brochure about the *Chambord* pattern lists a steak set and labels it as a 'Bird or Steak Set', thus suggesting two purposes for one item. Haviland china also made a game set consisting of a bird platter, individual bird plates, and a sauce boat and stand.

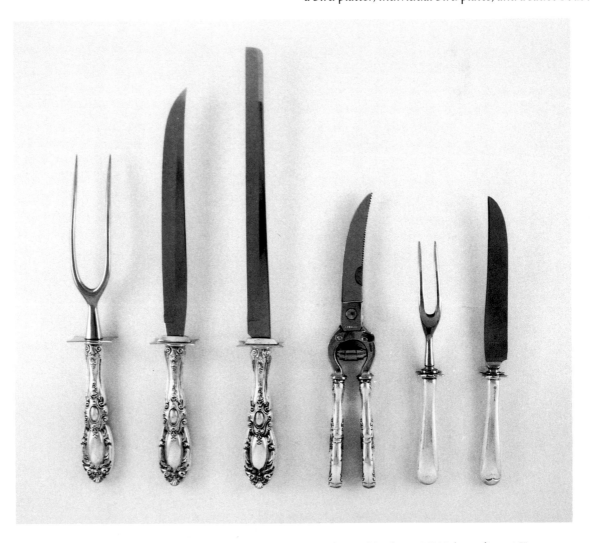

Figure 3.13, Carving Sets: Towle's *King Richard*, fork, 11 1/4", and knife, 14 9/32"; ham slicer, 15"; poultry shears 7"; Tuttle's *Hannah Hull* steak set, fork, 8 3/8", and knife, 9 15/16".

The small carving set by Tuttle in *Hannah Hull* (shown in Figure 3.13) includes a knife and fork and is useful for smaller cuts of meat. Hannah Hull was a real person in America's past. Her father was the first treasurer of the United States and the pattern was named after her. The pattern first appeared in 1927 and was made by Tuttle, now a division of Wallace Silversmiths. One interesting aspect of Tuttle sterling is that when each piece was made it contained a cartouch with the initials of the president of the United States in office at that time. This practice allows collectors to accurately place a reasonable date on the age of the item. This has been done since 1927 when Calvin Coolidge was president and the pattern was introduced.

Kirk's carving accessories, as taken from their 1938 catalog, included the following:

Roast Carvers, including Knives, Forks, and Steels,
Poultry Carvers, including Knives, Forks, and Steels,
Game Carvers, including Knives, Forks, and Steels,
   and Steak Carvers, including Knives, Forks, and
Steels. All of the items on the list have guards on
   the forks and knives.
Steak Carvers, without guards, including Knives, Forks,
   and steels,
Game Shears, 10 1/2", and a Roast Holder, 9 1/2".

Figure 3.14: A French bird plate by Limoges and a platter paired with Gorham's *Strasbourg* bird set, fork, 11", and knife, 11 7/8", and with Continental squab holders, 4".

Cheese Forks

Cheese forks have two tines, and one of the tines is relatively large for slicing or cutting the cheese and then assisting in picking up the slice. Cheese forks are relatively rare items as they are found in only a few patterns. Many old lists of Gorham patterns include the item, but it is seldom seen. Reed and Barton also made the forks as did a number of other manufacturers. These forks are a welcome addition to the buffet cheese platter, and they easily serve sliced cold meats.

Figure 3.15, Cheese Fork: Reed and Barton's *Francis I*, 6 7/16".

Cold Meat Forks

Cold meat forks are usually large forks, used to serve meat. All the examples shown have four tines. The forks come in a variety of sizes and should be chosen in an appropriate size for the meat being served; if the utensil dwarfs the meat it will be clumsy and ineffective in serving. In Figure 3.16, featuring the *Strasbourg* forks, the largest fork is the fork that is currently in production. When it is teamed with a tablespoon, another salad set can easily be assembled. The next fork with the beautiful piercing is called the 'Cold Meat Fork, Extra' in a 1911 Gorham catalog. The next fork with what appears to be a wide cutting tine is the 'Large Size Cold Meat Fork'. The last fork, the 'Small Cold Meat Fork', is best used with cold cuts or on the buffet table for thin sliced meats or cheese. The Gorham *Lancaster* example also shows the three size variations available with these forks. On the left of this figure, the Whiting *Louis XV* forks are shown in just two sizes, small and large.

Figure 3.16, Cold Meat Forks: Whiting's *Louis XV*, small, 6 1/2", and large, 7 1/2"; Gorham's *Lancaster*, small, 6 11/32", medium, 7 1/16", and large, 8 11/32"; *Strasbourg*, currently-produced, 8 1/2", large and pierced, 8 3/16", medium, 7 1/4", and small, 6 5/16".

The second illustration, Figure 3.17, shows the size variation in cold meat forks produced by a variety of manufacturers. All of the forks are approximately the same size except for the two examples in Durgin's *Dauphin*. The *Grand Colonial* cold meat fork by Wallace is smaller but still a very useful size. If the meat being served appears to dwarf the fork, the salad serving fork can easily be substituted for the smaller fork. Next is an example from Reed and Barton in *Francis I*, which is the smaller of two forks offered in that pattern. In *Grand Baroque*, a very popular modern pattern, the cold meat fork has a delicate edge that is beautifully pierced. Gorham's *Crown Baroque* is massive and beautifully detailed. The tines gently turn in, allowing one to pick up a small piece of meat. The next two forks are in Durgin's *Dauphin*. The first fork is an unusually large fork that can be used for serving

roast sliced turkey and presliced roast beef from large round platters at large buffet gatherings. The next fork is called a cold meat fork, or a large size individual fish fork. It is interesting to see how many functions some pieces of silver can be called upon to perform, while a catalog quickly confirms that original purpose or purposes. Stieff's *Corsage* has wide tines on both sides of the fork. Towle's *King Richard* had the typical tine pattern associated with cold meat forks from Towle. The last fork, with the grape decoration, is especially appropriate to California where so many grapes are grown. Items in this pattern called *Margeaux* by Towle were available for a time within the 1980s. This pattern resembles the pattern *Grape*, introduced in 1895 by Dominick and Haff.

Figure 3.17, Cold Meat Forks: Wallace's *Grand Colonial*, 8"; Reed and Barton's *Francis I*, small, 7 7/8"; Wallace's *Grand Baroque*, 8 3/16"; Gorham's *Crown Baroque*, 8 9/16"; Durgin's *Dauphin*, large, 9 5/16", and small, 7 11/32"; Stieff's *Corsage*, 7 27/32"; Towle's *King Richard*, 8 1/16"; and *Margeaux*, 7 7/8".

Fish Forks, Knives, & Sets

Fish sets are two-piece sets consisting of a knife, referred to as a blade, and a fork. The fork is usually larger than the cold meat fork, and the knife is usually smaller than a crumb knife. Fish forks and knives are essential for serving a whole poached or baked fish on the buffet table. The fork gently lifts the cooked fish onto the knife or blade and helps hold the fish until it is served. These two pieces come in two sizes, large and small, from most companies. In Figure 3.18 two examples from Gorham in their *Strasbourg* pattern are shown. They are very similar in design, but careful inspection will reveal a difference in the design at the end of the handles where they attach to the tines or the blades. Here one can find additional scrolls so typical of the *Strasbourg* design. On the right, an impressive set in Whiting's *Louis XV* is shown. Notice the beautiful wave-like design in the silver of both pieces. It is truly a masterful fish set.

Figure 3.18, Fish Forks, Knives, and Sets: Gorham's *Strasbourg*, fork, 8 11/16", and knife, 11 13/16"; fork, 8 7/16", and knife, 11 3/8"; Whiting's *Louis XV*, fork, 9 5/16", and knife, 12 1/2".

Figure 3.19 shows a large size and a small size fish set. The large set, in Kirk's *Repoussé* has a beautiful blade with a fanciful edge. The fork has five tines. On the right of this figure is a Gorham *Lancaster* small fish set. The differences between these two is size. The choice of which set to use depends on the size of the fish and the dish in which it is served. In the center of this picture are three single fish blades: the small blade in Whiting's *Louis XV*, a sterling hollow-handled piece with a stainless blade (note the fish design in the blade), and a blade in Durgin's *Dauphin*. Durgin appears to have made just one size fish blade in *Dauphin*, according to the lists appearing in Maryanne Dolan's text, *1830s-1990s American Sterling Silver Flatware* (1993).

Figure 3.19, Fish Forks, Knives, and Sets: Kirk's *Repoussé* knife, 11 7/16", and fork, 9 1/16"; Whiting's *Louis XV*, small knife, 9 1/2"; Stieff's *Corsage*, knife, 10 1/16"; Durgin's *Dauphin*, knife, 10 3/4"; Gorham's *Lancaster*, fork, 7 1/16", and knife, 10 3/8".

Two examples of fish blades from before the Civil War are shown in Figure 3.20. Turner (1971) states that small and large fish blades were introduced in approximately 1820, well before these two examples. The first blade, on the left with the twisted handle and beautifully cut blade, is marked only "Bailey and Company." In Dorothy T. Rainwater's text, *Encyclopedia of American Silver Manufacturers, Third Edition Revised* (1986), there is a mention of a Bailey and Company in a discussion of Bailey, Banks and Biddle, the Philadelphia jeweler. The company was known as Bailey and Company from 1846 to 1878. A pair of pie knifes with this same mark can be found in Figure 3.36b. While very similar, the design is different and the cartouch is vacant, without a monogram, a rarity in such an old piece of silver. Further review of Rainwater's text shows a silversmith named George B. Sharp who worked for Bailey from 1848 to 1850. He marked his sterling with the following mark:

This type of mark was used by only a few early American silversmiths. Rainwater related that Sharp also included a statement that "All Silver Ware sold by them manufactured on the premises—Assayed by J. C. Booth, Esq., of the U. S. mint." The second item in Kirk's *Mayflower* has a beautifully executed scroll design engraved into the blade.

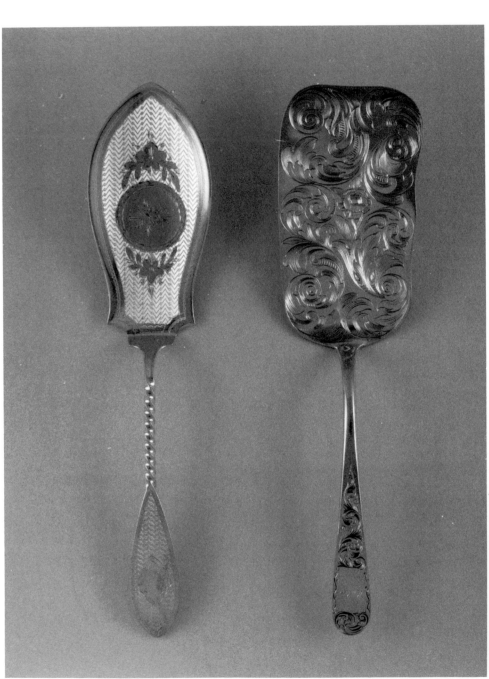

Figure 3.20, Fish Knives: Bailey and Company, unknown pattern, knife, 11 1/4"; and Kirk's *Mayflower*, knife, 11".

Lemon Forks, Peelers, & Servers

Lemon forks are another tool for use at the tea table, usually smaller than pickle forks, with flared outside tines. At one time the lemon fork was considered so necessary an item that it was included at each place setting in the southern part of the United States. Today the forks are useful for serving a myriad of food items at cocktail parties. Some forks have two tines, others have three.

All of the items in Figure 3.21 can be compared and contrasted to show the various forms of lemon fork, as executed by various manufacturers. The first two examples are by Kirk, one with a long handle and the other with a short handle. In another twist, Kirk shows a lemon fork with two tines, and gives it double billing—as both a lemon fork and a butter fork. The next two examples , Schofield's *Baltimore Rose* and Stieff's *Corsage*, show how these two manufacturers have made similar, but not identical, lemon forks. Note how the tines are different sizes and shapes. Three examples by Gorham, in *Buttercup, Crown Baroque*, and *King Edward*, are small with widely spread tines. International's *Royal Danish* has a handle about the length of the Gorham examples, but its tines are not as widely spread apart. Wallace's examples in *Grand Colonial* and *Rose Point* give yet another variation; they are the largest of the lemon forks. *Burgundy*, an example made by Reed and Barton, is unique with a pierced section.

Orange peelers and citrus knives were developed during the 1890s to take advantage of the tremendously large citrus crops. Silver manufacturers made a number of silver items to call attention to the use of citrus fruit. Peelers, as exemplified in Figure 3.21, combined a sterling handle with a hook-shaped end. The hook peeled the orange skin into sections, thus assisting in removing the skin so that the edible fruit could be more easily accessed. The example in the figure is Durgin's *Bead*. To use an orange peeler, hold the orange as if it were still attached to the stem upon which it grew. Then insert the hook of the peeler and draw it down to the bottom of the orange. Repeat this until the orange has been scored into a number of sections, depending upon the size of the orange, and then remove the skin to enjoy the tasty orange. Citrus knives were all silver, and most had serrated edges for cutting and two tines for picking up the sliced fruit (For further discussion see Fruit Knives, Individual, Figure 1.34).

Lemon servers are very rare utensils as they were made by only a few companies. Most were larger than a jelly serving spoon, but usually pierced. These items allowed the user to lift a lemon slice from a plate. Some lemon servers had two small tines at the end of the blade to spear the lemon slice before picking it up and serving it. These items are easily confused with small croquette servers, which usually had a similar shape.

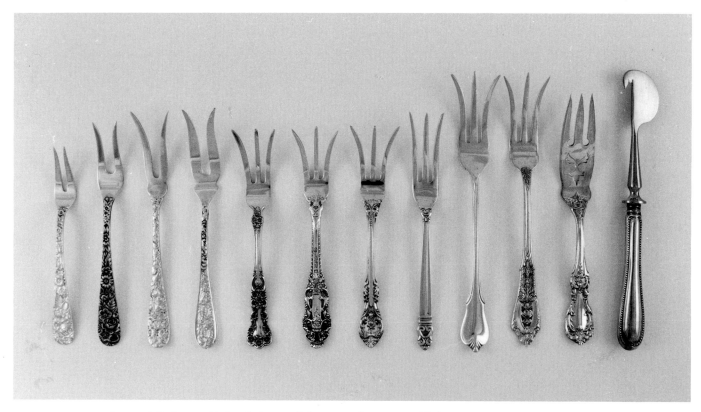

Figure 3.21, Lemon Forks, Peelers, and Servers: Kirk's *Repoussé* forks, small, 4", and large, 4 1/2"; Schofield's *Baltimore Rose* fork, 4 11/16"; Stieff's *Corsage* fork, 4 3/4"; Gorham's *Buttercup* fork, 4 3/8"; Gorham's *Crown Baroque* fork, 4 3/8"; Gorham's *King Edward* fork, 4 3/8"; International's *Royal Danish* fork, 4 11/16"; Wallace's *Grand Colonial* fork, 5 1/2"; Wallace's *Rosepoint* fork, 5 3/8"; Reed and Barton's *Burgundy* fork, 5"; and Durgin's *Bead* orange peeler, 5 9/16".

Lettuce Forks, Spoons, & Sets

Lettuce forks and spoons are long-handled servers. The tines on many forks are beautifully pierced and the bowls of the spoons compliment the size of the forks. Lettuce forks and spoons are very useful for serving salad greens or a spinach-mushroom salad served in a beautiful cut glass bowl. In Figure 3.22 are three sets fork and spoon sets that were manufactured by Gorham. The first example is in *Lancaster*, the second in *Cambridge*, and the third in *Strasbourg*. All of these pieces are very similar with the exception of the stamped design in the bowl of the *Lancaster* spoon and the piercing between the tines on the *Strasbourg* fork.

Some manufacturers did not make a salad serving spoon, but collectors can find another fork and pair the two together to form a serving set or use a chocolate muddler with the lettuce fork to form a set. Examples of lettuce forks without accompanying spoons include, Durgin's *Dauphin*, Kirk's *Repoussé*, Stieff's *Corsage*, Gorham's *Chantilly*, and the two different examples in Whiting's *Louis XV*. Take note of the different handles on the Whiting examples. While the tines are the same, almost half of the handle on one of the examples was left plain.

Using these pieces with salad dressing is not advised because both vinegar and mayonnaise react with the silver almost instantaneously to cause ugly stains that are difficult to remove. Gold wash on the tines and bowls will help cut the possible reaction of dressing and vinegar. Serving the dressing in a cruet or small bowl saves cleaning the silver.

Figure 3.22, Lettuce Forks and Spoons: Durgin's *Dauphin*, fork, 8 3/4"; Kirk's *Repoussé*, fork, 8 3/4"; Gorham's *Lancaster*, fork, 9 3/4", and spoon, 9 3/8"; *Cambridge*, fork, 9 3/8", and spoon, 9 3/8"; *Strasbourg*, fork, 9 1/4", and spoon, 9 1/4"; Stieff's *Corsage*, fork, 9 3/8"; *Chantilly*, fork, 8 1/2"; Whiting's *Louis XV*, fork, 9 1/8"; fork (with plain section), 9 5/16".

Pickle-Olive Forks, Spoons, & Sets

Pickle/olive forks cannot be accurately identified by counting the tines. At one time Gorham used three tines and currently uses two as shown by the forks in the *Decor, Crown Baroque,* and *Chantilly* patterns. In Figure 3.23 a they are contrasted with the three-tined *Strasbourg* fork. The two forks from Wallace, *Rosepoint* and *Grand Colonial,* have two tines. There really is no difference between a pickle and an olive fork. Manufacturers simply labeled some as one and some as the other. In the illustration Figure 3.23a showing *King Richard,* there are both an olive and a pickle fork. Towle has made a distinct function for each. The example in Whiting's *Imperial Queen* has small barbs on each of the two tines to assist in holding the olive or pickle slice.

Please refer to the section where butter pick forks are shown (Figures 3.8, 3.9, and 3.10) for further discussion of pickle/butter pick-forks, which are confused with pickle forks. A quick comparison may help to identify the purpose any fork in question. If your sterling is by Gorham, and the fork has two tines, check the back of the item. In the 1930s or 1940s Gorham began placing their name on the back of the fork, and if you find it there your fork may be a pickle fork. If your fork has a maker's mark and flared tines, usually the fork is a butter pick-fork.

Figure 3.23a, Pickle-Olive Forks, Spoons, and Sets: Wallace's *Rosepoint,* 5 9/16"; *Grand Colonial,* 5 9/16"; Reed and Barton's *Marlborough,* 5 1/2"; Gorham's *Cambridge,* 5 11/16"; *Strasbourg,* 5 25/32"; Reed and Barton's *Grand Renaissance,* 6"; Whiting's *Imperial Queen,* 6 1/4"; Durgin's *Dauphin* (long-handled olive/pickle fork), 7 5/16"; Stieff's *Corsage,* 6 1/16"; Towle's *King Richard,* Pickle/Olive, 6 1/8"; Olive, 6 1/32"; Gorham's *Crown Baroque,* 5 13/16"; *Decor,* 6 3/4"; *Chantilly,* 5 13/16"; and International's *Royal Danish,* 5 7/8".

In Figure 3.23b the illustration compares long and short handled olive/pickle sets. The first pair of examples, in Whiting's *Louis XV*, typify the sets in Whiting. Both of the forks have the barbed tines as seen in Figure 3.23a and both also are beautifully pierced in the bowls of the spoons. The next three examples are not complete as they are missing either a fork or a spoon. The first fork, in Alvin's *Raleigh*, the Gorham *Cambridge* pierced spoon, and the fork in *Buttercup* are typical pieces. The last two sets in Gorham's *Lancaster* allow close comparison between large and small styled sets.

Figure 3.23b, Forks, Spoons and Sets: Whiting's *Louis XV*, short fork, 6 7/32", short spoon, 6 3/8", long fork, 8 15/16", long spoon, 9"; Alvin's *Raleigh*, 8 1/2"; Gorham's *Cambridge*, 8 1/2"; *Buttercup*, 8 1/8"; *Lancaster*, long spoon, 8 11/16", long fork, 8 3/8", short spoon, 5 13/16", and short fork, 5 3/4".

These six forks in Figure 3.24, four of which are of Baltimore origin, provide additional examples of the variety that can be found in pickle forks. The long handled Stieff's *Rose* is magnificent. The barbs found on the end of the tines are unique. Note the twist in the last fork in this figure. The *King's* pattern is typical of pickle forks, as is the example in Rogers, Lunt, and Bolan's *Pynchon*.

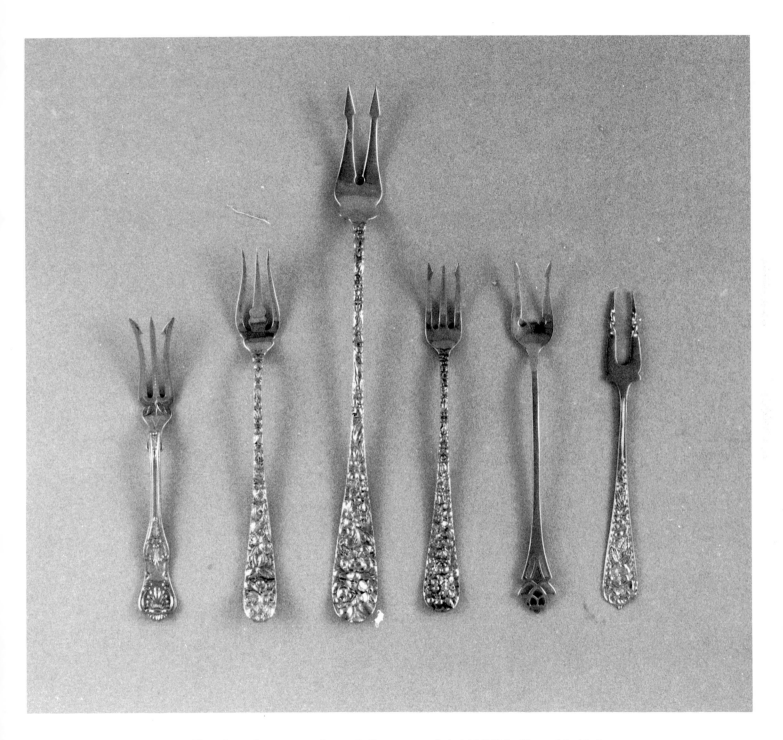

Figure 3.24 Pickle Forks: Unknown manufacturer's *Kings* pattern, fork, 4 15/16"; Jenkins and Jenkins', 5 3/16"; Stieff's *Rose*, long fork, 8 11/16", short fork, 5 5/8"; Rogers, Lunt and Bolan's *Pynchon*, fork, 5 3/4"; unknown maker and pattern, fork, 5 3/16".

Piccalilli and Chow-Chow Forks, Spoons, and Sets

Piccalilli was a popular sweet relish made at the close of summer with green tomatoes. Our forefathers seldom wasted anything, and what better way to save the remaining green tomatoes before the first frost than in a piccalilli? The piccalilli sets, consisting of a fork and a spoon, were not made by all manufacturers, or in all patterns, but Tiffany and Towle did make them. What Towle appears to have done is use a long-handled olive spoon and a long-handled olive fork, and packaged them together as a piccalilli set. By not piercing the olive spoon, it appeared that the manufacturer had developed a new item.

Chow-Chow was made with a number of vegetables cooked in a mustard sauce. Tiffany made chow-chow sets consisting of a fork and a spoon. These sets, like the Tiffany example in Figure 3.25, were shorter than piccalilli sets. Note the very fine, delicately pierced bowl on the spoon and the almost hairlike piercing below the tines of the fork in the Tiffany pieces. Towle appears to have made their sets using the short-handled pickle fork and an unpierced short-handled olive spoon.

Figure 3.25, Piccalilli and Chow-Chow Forks, Spoons, and Sets: Towle's *Georgian*, fork, 5 15/16"; Tiffany's *Tomato Vine*, Spoon, 6 1/16'; Fork, 6 5/16".

The example in Whiting's *Louis XV* in Figure 3.28 is a long-handled salad set. This set can be used in a large salad bowl on a buffet table. By showing the regular set in the same figure one can easily compare and contrast the two sizes of salad sets, regular and long.

Figure 3.28 (top to bottom): Whiting's *Louis XV*, regular-handled fork, 8 7/8", regular-handled spoon, 9 1/8", long-handled spoon, 12", and long-handled fork, 8 7/8".

Sardine and Anchovy Forks, Helpers, and Lifters

Sardine forks were made by most manufacturers, a few with long handles. At one time sardines were an important part of the American diet because they were among the first food items to be canned. Thus, they were a status symbol in the latter part of the Victorian era. Sardines have been over-fished and are less available today, but at the height of their popularity silversmiths created some beautiful examples. *Lancaster* [note the two styles in this pattern], two forks in *Louis XV* [again, note one fork is longer], *New Art*, and *Chantilly*, a sardine helper *Francis I*, and sardine tongs *Louis XV* (see Figure 3.77). Some of the first sardine forks that were made have been found with a master serving fork and twelve individual forks. Forks found from the early sets have the same tine pattern as the smaller *Lancaster* sardine fork. The Whiting examples in *Louis XV* show how manufacturers changed the shape of some items over a period of time. Today the forks lend themselves to serving special Armenian or middle eastern delicacies—dolma, or stuffed grape leaves. Even Kirk's bacon fork was at one time labeled a long handled sardine fork.

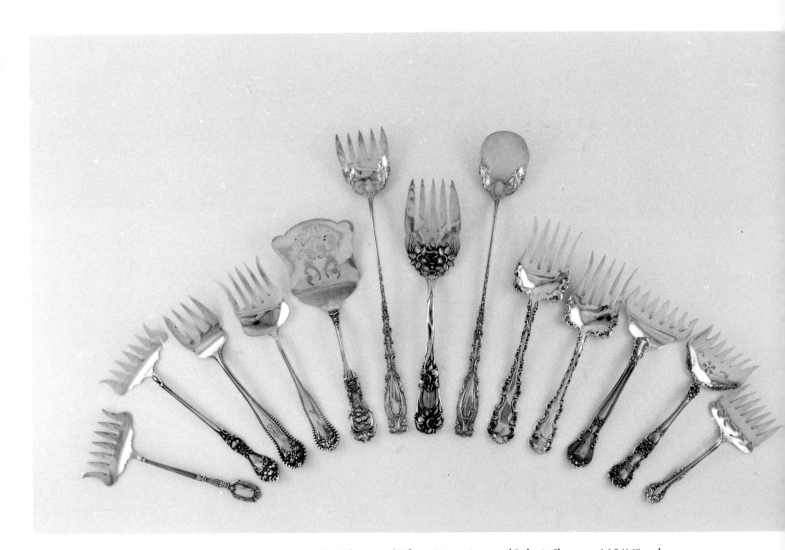

Figure 3.29: Sardine Forks, Helpers, and Lifters: Rogers, Lunt and Bolen's *Sheraton*, 4 15/16"; unknown manufacturer, unknown floral pattern, 5 1/2". Gorham's *Lancaster*, old style, 5 7/16"; new style, 5 1/2"; Reed and Barton's *Francis I* (lifter), 6 1/8"; Frank Whiting's *Josephine*, (long-handled fork), 8 1/8"; Durgin's *New Art*, 6 3/4"; Frank Whiting's *Josephine*, (long-handled spoon), 8 3/16"; Whiting's *Louis XV*, Style #1, 6 1/8", and Style #2, 5 5/8"; Gorham's *Chantilly*, 5 1/8", and *Buttercup*, 5"; and Alvin's *Florentine*, 4 1/8".

In this figure the Gorham *Medallion* and the Wood and Hughes examples are the oldest items. The other three examples show typical Sardine forks. The Wood and Hughes example typifies early sardine forks.

Figure 3.30a, Sardine Forks: Gorham's *Medallion*, sardine fork, 5 5/8"; Jenkins and Jenkins, sardine fork, 5 15/16"; Schofield's *Baltimore Rose*, sardine fork 6"; Wood and Hughes, sardine fork, 5 3/8"; and unknown pattern, Schofield mark, anchovy fork, 4 3/4".

Figure 3.30b: This handpainted, three-piece Haviland sardine box and tray is beautifully decorated. The area at the bottom of the box appears to be designed for resting a sardine fork or sardine helper. A three-piece set in this Haviland china pattern is rare.

Spinach Fork

Spinach forks are long, pointed, large-tined forks. They were made in very few patterns, and as such they are very rare. The example shown is in *Dresden* by Whiting. This pattern is listed as "n.l.p." in the *Jeweler's Keystone*, which means "not line pattern," or not a complete pattern line. This indicates that the pattern was incomplete; Whiting offered only the serving pieces. The best example of this is *New Art*, introduced by Durgin in 1899. There were a number of pieces in serving and place piece but not a complete line of flatware. Some of the pieces featured the iris plant, and were later incorporated into the *Iris* pattern when it was introduced in 1904.

Figure 3.32, Spinach Fork: Whiting's *Dresden*, 9 11/16".

Toast or Bread Fork/Server

Toast forks and servers are left over from a bygone era when loaves of bread were smaller. The wide toast fork was inserted into the loaf of bread steadying the bread so it could be sliced with a serrated bread knife. Both items were used at the same time, much like a carving set.

In the photograph, the *Lancaster* fork is representative of Gorham's toast fork as seen in catalog pictures and original copies of the design patent. Durgin's toast forks are almost identically shaped on all patterns. The reverse of Durgin's toast forks are plain and devoid of any design. Only a maker's mark and the word "Sterling" appears, with the selling jeweler's mark visible. In Figure 3.33c and 3.33d, the jeweler's mark shows. In this case it is "B. B. & B. Co.," likely an abbreviation of Bailey, Banks and Biddle Company. Towle also made a bread fork that could be used to serve toast. It was three-tined and similar to Gorham's toast forks.

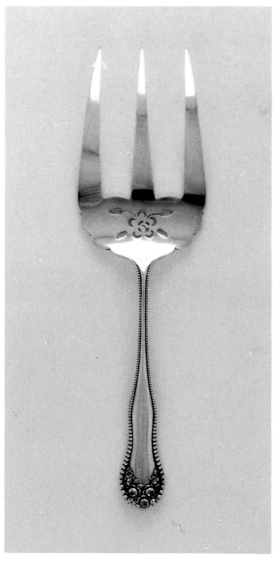

Figure 3.33a, Toast or Bread Fork/Server: Gorham's *Lancaster*, 8 7/16".

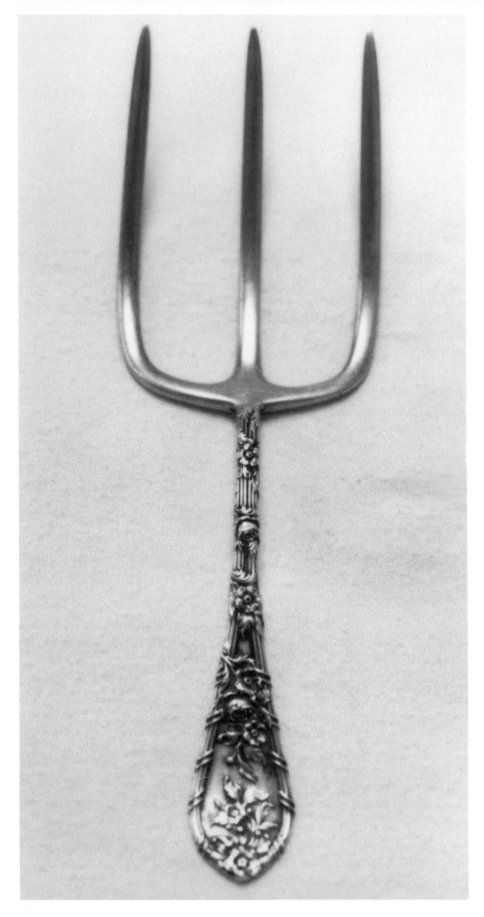

Figures 3.33b, Toast or Bread Fork/Server: Durgin's *Dauphin, 6 3/4". Courtesy of Hank Thompson*

One Gorham catalog illustrating *Chantilly* shows the asparagus fork listed both as an asparagus and a toast fork. This double name explains why *Chantilly* forks can be found that can have two types of tines—one widely pierced (more likely the toast fork) and the other having delicate piercing between the three large tines (the asparagus fork). Refer to Figure 3-4 for this example. Labeling the fork with two jobs allowed Gorham to offer a greater variety of items.

Today toast forks work to serve various breakfast breads or rolls. Croissants are easily served with a toast fork.

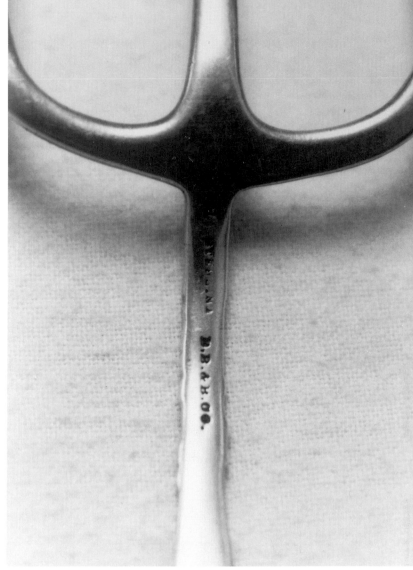

Figure 3.33c, Toast or Bread Fork/Server: Durgin's *Dauphin* pattern, 6 3/4". *Courtesy of Hank Thompson*

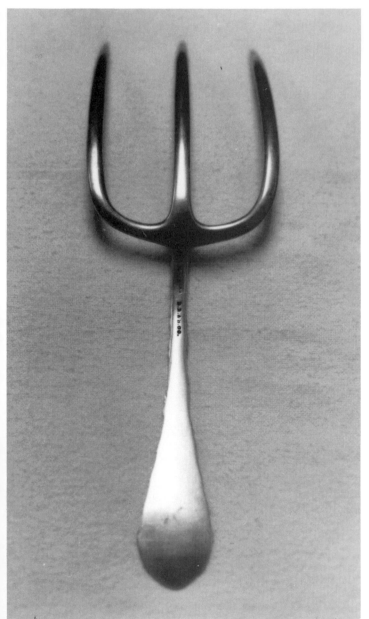

Figure 3.33d, Toast or Bread Fork/Server: Durgin's *Dauphin*, 6 3/4". *Courtesy of Hank Thompson*

Vegetable Forks, Spoons, and Sets

Vegetable forks and spoons are used either singly or in combination for serving cooked vegetables. This picture shows vegetable forks by Reed and Barton in *Francis I* and Gorham's *Strasbourg*, and vegetable spoons in *Buttercup* and *Baronial* by Gorham. Note the difference in the shapes of the two spoons' bowls. The reader can easily distinguish how the *Baronial* piece could serve items with juice or gravy due to the shape of the bowl, while the *Buttercup* piece could easily serve casseroles, crepes and enchiladas. The fork in *Francis I* has been labeled a 'Serving Fork, Large' and also a 'Vegetable Fork'. Gorham made a set, but not in all patterns, and the fork was larger than a Salad Serving Fork. Other silver companies may have made the same servers, but they are also very difficult to locate. The *Strasbourg* fork paired with a *Strasbourg* berry spoon makes a fantastic serving set. In the center of this figure Stieff's *Corsage* Vegetable Spoon is featured. It is pierced to allow the vegetables to be served in their own liquid, thus assuring that the vegetables will be hot.

Figure 3.34, Vegetable Forks, Spoons, and Sets: Gorham's *Strasbourg*, fork, 8 3/4"; Reed and Barton's *Francis I*, fork, 9 1/8"; Stieff's *Corsage*, spoon, 8 3/8"; Gorham's *Buttercup*, spoon, 10 1/16", and *Baronial*, spoon, 9 7/8".

Knives

Butter Knives

Butter knives that are all silver (A.S.) can be easily identified by a bend at the base of the cutting edge where the handle joins the cutting edge; hollow-handled (H.H.) implements, on the other hand, have somewhat fancy blades. Both kinds of butter knives are still in production. These knives are excellent for serving some types of cream cheese and nut spreads and of course, butter. The illustration shows both hollow-handled and all-silver types of spreaders. Almost without exception, sterling all-silver butter knives are basically flat, with a bend where the blade attaches to the handle. This bend allows the handle and the base of the blade to rest on a surface. The bend facilitates picking up the butter knife. Some silver-plated knives are twisted, with the handle resting flat on the table and the blade at a ninety degree angle to the handle. The only exceptions to this appear in coin silver, or in some patterns that appeared shortly after the Civil War.

In some old sterling patterns, there is a pickle fork and a pickle knife. The pickle knife is usually a smaller version of the butter knife and it was used to sample the relishes and pickles which were an important part of the American diet, especially for those people who lived in the colder climates where fresh vegetables and fruit were almost impossible to come by during the winter. Old pickle knives are approximately the same size as the A.S. Butter Knife currently produced in many patterns. The two pieces in Figure 1.12 are found in Gorham's *Strasbourg*, *Lancaster*, and Whiting's *Louis XV*. The Whiting's *Louis XV* pickle knife is completely different because of its shape.

Some collectors have collected the relatively common large butter knives and use them in place of hard-to-find flat fish knives. Stieff listed its butter knife as either a butter knife or a fish knife. In Figure 3.35 the *Lancaster* piece is the knife that was collected as a fish knife. Again, the Whiting Company is an exception. Their fish knives (Figure 1.28) are identical to the above two butter knives except that they are flat.

Butter knives are larger than individual butter spreaders. Individual butter spreaders were made in two sizes by some companies and in three sizes by others. All-silver knives and those with hollow handles had a variety of blade styles. Some hollow handled knives even had sterling blades. For further discussion on this aspect of individual butter knives, please see Figures 1.31, 1.32, and 1.33.

In Figure 3.35, the first three hollow-handled knives on the left were made by Gorham in the following patterns: *Strasbourg*, *La Scala*, and *Crown Baroque*. The first example has a blade style that balances with the design, and the next two have identical blades. On the right of this figure another Gorham example of a hollow-handled spreader in *King Edward* has a third style blade. This blade style again complements the design of the sterling handle. The last hollow-handled example is Towle's *King Richard*. It too has a completely different blade, which harmonizes with the design.

The remainder of the knives in Figure 3.35 are all sterling. The fourth from the left, Durgin's *Dauphin*, is the only example to have the flowers flow from the handle onto the blade of the knife. The example from Stieff in *Corsage* has a somewhat scalloped design. The large Gorham *Lancaster* example with the fully scalloped design on the top of the cutting blade is magnificent. The next two examples, from Whiting in *Louis XV*, show two knives that can be used depending upon the size of the container. The next sample, from Wallace in its *Peony* design, is highly collectable as a floral pattern. Reed and Barton's *Marlborough* knife blade appears to float right into the design of the handle. The last piece, Wallace's *Grand Colonial*, is a large server and typical of butter knives.

Figure 3.35, Butter Knives: Gorham's *Strasbourg*, hollow-handled, 6 11/16"; *La Scala*, 6 7/8"; *Crown Baroque*, 7"; Durgin's *Dauphin*, 6 7/8"; Stieff's *Corsage*, 7 1/8"; Gorham's *Lancaster*, 7 5/8"; Whiting's *Louis XV*, large, 7 3/4", and small, 7"; Wallace's *Peony*, 6 7/8"; Reed and Barton's *Marlborough*, 6 15/16"; Wallace's *Grand Colonial*, 6 15/16"; Gorham's *La Scala*, hollow-handled 6 7/8; and Towle's *King Richard*, 6 5/8".

Figure 3.36a, All Silver:
Top row, cake or pastry knives: Reed and Barton's *Francis I* (current), 9 9/16", jelly roll knife, 10 1/8"; Gorham's *Lancaster* (Shreve), 8 1/4"; Alvin's *Bridal Rose*, 9 3/16"; slightly lower is Gorham's *Lancaster* (Vanderslice), 9 5/16"; Durgin's *Dauphin*, 8 3/8"; and slightly lower is Whiting's *King Edward*, 9 5/32".
Bottom row, pie knives: Gorham's *Lancaster*, 9 1/8"; Whiting's *Louis XV*, 9 1/8"; and an unknown pattern marked "Coin,"   8 1/4".

The markings found on the two pieces shown here can be traced to George Sharp, a silversmith who worked for Bailey and Company, currently Bailey, Banks and Biddle. See Figure 3.20 for an example of Bailey's mark. The beautiful engraving and the cartouch for the monogram used in the examples is typical for silver of this age. It is uncommon to find a beautiful example without a monogram, like one of the Pie Servers in this figure.

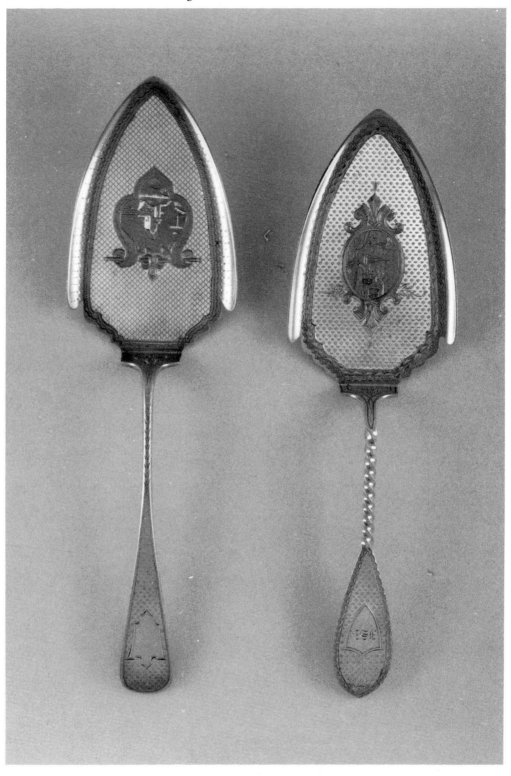

Figure, 3.36b, All-Silver Pie Servers: Bailey and Co., unknown patterns, 11 7/16" and 11 1/4".

Cake, Pie & Pastry Knives, Plated or Stainless

Cake, pie, and pastry knives can have all-silver blades, pierced or not, or stainless steel blades currently made with a slight bend at the base of the handle. Currently, most manufacturers only have the stainless steel version available, with a stainless blade fitted into a sterling hollow handle. One exception as shown in Figure 3.36 is Reed and Barton's all silver *Francis I* pie/cake knife. All of the above items serve cake, pie or pastry with ease.

It seems that the *King Edward* knife in the illustration may be a jelly roll knife, especially when compared with the *Francis I* jelly roll knife. The reverse of the *King Edward* piece has the patent date, April 23, 1901. In the past this feature was used only for the first sixteen years of a new pattern. Today it is no longer necessary to place design patent numbers on silver, or to indicate the date of the design; only the manufacturer is indicated. Jelly roll knives are slender and frequently the length of the blade is delicately pierced. Most of the jelly roll knives were made by Reed and Barton. All of these all-silver knives are wonderful for serving cheesecake, or other rich desserts for which a small serving is adequate. Notice the two examples in Gorham's *Lancaster* with different blades. One is backstamped with the name of G. Shreve and Co., and the other with Vanderslice and Co. Both of these items were made in the jewelers' factories. For other samples by the same jewelers see Figures 3.89 and 3.90.

In the bottom row of figure three examples of pie knives by Gorham in *Lancaster*, Whiting's *Louis XV*, and a coin example with beautiful engraving upon the blade and handle are shown.

Figure 3.37 presents the variety of pie and cake knives that have been made using a sterling handle and various blades. Some blades may be silver-plated, or stainless flat or stainless with a bend. On the bottom, Gorham's *King Edward* and *Crown Baroque* pastry servers are located. This type of blade would be useful for serving Danish pastry. Kirk's catalog shows an item similar in shape to a pastry server with a stainless blade and a sterling handle. The shape is more oval, and Kirk labels this implement as an Egg Server.

Figure 3.37, Pie or Pastry Knives:
Top row, new-style stainless blades: Gorham's *Crown Baroque*, 11 3/16"; Stieff's *Corsage*, 10 1/4"; Gorham's *King Edward*, 10 1/8"; Towle's *King Richard*, 10 7/16"; and Wallace's *Grand Colonial*, 10 7/8".
Bottom row, plated, flat stainless, and stainless steel: Gorham's silver-plated blade, *Lancaster*, 9 7/8", and *Strasbourg*, 9 7/8"; Stieff's flat stainless, *Corsage*, 9 7/8"; Gorham's stainless pastry servers, *King Edward*, 10 1/8" and *Crown Baroque*, 10 5/8".

Cheese Knives, Servers, Slicers, Picks, Planes, Cleavers, & Pronged Servers

Cheese knives and servers come in a variety of shapes: spade-shaped, cleaver-shaped, prong-shaped, plane-shaped, flat or fanciful. One example uses a wire to cut the cheese. Cheese items have been a part of silver services for many years, and currently several forms of these items are available from a number of manufacturers.

At one time the prong-shaped cheese knife was considered a place piece. There are two examples of this item and they vary slightly in the prong area. The complete Victorian home would need a dozen in order to use one at each place setting. The main reason cheese knives did not become place pieces is that Victorian society frowned upon diners placing knives in their mouths. It would appear that the place pieces did not become popular and was relegated to being a serving implement.

There are a number or variations on the cheese knife form. The large *Strasbourg* piece has a cutting edge for slicing the cheese and the teeth to pick up and serve the cheese. A few early examples of cheese knives and tines from about the time of the Civil War show pieces in which the blade portion has a quarter turn, allowing the handle to rest on the table. The *Louis XV* example by Whiting has three small prongs for picking up the sliced cheese, quite different from other toothed versions. The *Lancaster* piece by Gorham shows the prongs at a different angle from either of the previous examples. Each cheese serving piece has a particular advantage, and no collection is really complete without one or more of these unusual implements.

The Gorham *Strasbourg* example on the right, with the bend in the blade, is a currently marked 'Cheese Knife'. At one time it was called the 'Cheese Server, Small'. The fancy example in Gorham's *Plymouth*, center, is called the 'Cheese Server, Large'. The cheese knives by Towle's *King Richard*, Gorham's *King Edward*, and *Crown Baroque* are in current production.

In the second row, two examples of cheese cleavers are shown. They were made by Gorham in the *Strasbourg* and *Buttercup* patterns. These items were available for a time, but no longer appear on the currently available list. Other companies are now using the same stainless blade so it seems possible they may be offered again.

Before stainless blades were made with a bend, they were made to lay straight, as seen in Stieff's *Corsage* and Wallace's *Grand Colonial*. Older examples had blades made in silver-plate.

The wire cheese cutter by Webb does not have a pattern name. It is meant to be held in the hand, and the cutting wire moves along the cheese wedge. As the cheese is cut it begins to fall and the two long, stainless tines catch the slice.

The all-silver example without a maker's mark is most likely an all-silver cheese server. The cheese pick is in the *Princess* pattern by Manchester. Today, this item is available in a number of current patterns. The last item, the cheese plane by Reed and Barton in *Francis I*, is one of the newest cheese serving items. Its blade is pulled over a brick of cheese and a thin slice is removed.

Figure 3.38, Cheese Knives, Servers, Slicers, Picks, Planes, Cleavers, and Pronged Servers:
Top row, cheese servers: Gorham's comb-top/pronged *Strasbourg*, 8 1/8" and 8"; Whiting's comb-top/pronged *Louis XV*, 7 17/32"; Gorham's comb-top/pronged *Lancaster*, 7 13/16"; Gorham's *Plymouth* large cheese server with a silver-plated blade, 7 1/8"; Towle's *King Richard*, 6 7/8"; Gorham's *King Edward*, 7", *Crown Baroque*, 7 1/4", and *Strasbourg*, 6 15/16".
Bottom row: Gorham's *Strasbourg* cheese cleaver, 6 11/32", and *Buttercup* cheese cleaver, 6 3/8"; Stieff's *Corsage* flat, stainless cheese server, 6 1/4", and *Grand Colonial* flat, stainless cheese server, 6 7/16"; Webb, unknown pattern, stainless wire cheese cutter, 8 5/8"; unknown manufacturer and unknown pattern, all sterling wire cutter, 5 7/8"; Manchester's *Princess*, pronged server, 7 5/8"; Reed and Barton's *Francis I*, cheese plane, 8 7/8".

Crumb Knives

A large blade with a straight, blunt side distinguishes a crumb knife. Two variations within the *Dauphin* pattern, are shown in the illustration, along with examples in Gorham's *Lancaster* and Whiting's *Louis XV*. The Whiting example has a unique edge and provides another variation in crumb knifes. The *Strasbourg* piece was purchased at Shreve and Company Jewelers in 1906 before the devastating San Francisco earthquake. The *Strasbourg*, *Buttercup*, and *Lancaster* examples show the variation from one manufacturer in a serving piece. The blade on the *Lancaster* piece carries the same marking that many of the pieces in that pattern have. The oldest piece is the Gorham's *Medallion* knife. Originally servants cleared the dishes and silverware from the table and then removed crumbs using the crumb knife from the heavy damask tablecloth. The maid then proceeded with serving the next course of the meal. Some silver patterns made a "dustpan" type of receptacle with a small brush to remove crumbs, or a dustpan paired with a crumb knife. Today crumb knives can be used to serve a main course like enchiladas, or dessert crepes.

Figure 3.39, Crumb Knives: Gorham's *Lancaster*, 12 5/8"; Durgin's *Dauphin*, 12 7/8", special edge, 12 7/16"; Whiting's *Louis XV*, 12 11/16"; Gorham's *Medallion*, 12 1/8"; Gorham's *Buttercup*, 11 1/2"; and *Strasbourg*, 11 1/2".

Jelly Knives

Jelly knives all have a somewhat sharp cutting edge in all sizes. The handle of the knife usually has a design which continues onto the knife blade in some patterns. They range in size from just over seven inches to over eight inches in length, with the blade commensurate with the length of the handle. At times some manufacturers made two sizes in jelly knives as shown in Gorham's *Lancaster*, others made three. Found in as many as three sizes, jelly knives were used to serve aspic jelly in days gone by. Everything from head cheese, based in aspic, to clear fruited jelly was served. Tiffany made an aspic slicer which was a large sickle shaped server. No other manufacturer seems to have made this sickle shaped item. Today the jelly knife, depending upon the shape, could be used to serve cheese cake and other desserts.

Figure 3.40, Jelly Knives: unknown manufacturer, unknown pattern, 7 31/32"; Towle's *Canterbury*, 7 1/4"; Gorham's *Strasbourg*, 6 15/16"; Wallace's *Rose*, 8"; Whiting's *Imperial Queen*, 8 1/4", and *Louis XV*, 8 15/16"; Gorham's *Lancaster*, 6 15/16" and 8 1/4".

Ice Cream Knives & Servers

Ice cream knives are either hollow-handled (H.H.) or all-silver (A.S.). The all-silver example in photograph Figure 3.41 of *Arlington* by Towle shows remarkable craftsmanship. The handle is cast in three pieces. The central portion, where the design is engraved on the blade, continues between two affixed floral handles. The floral handles are attached to create a "sandwich type" serving piece. The H.H. *Strasbourg* piece with the stainless blade is very useful to serve brick ice cream, as is Stieff's *Corsage*. The example in Whiting's *Louis XV* is truly magnificent and regal. The flat handle of the *Buttercup* and *Lancaster* pieces shows the beautiful work of the designer.

Reed and Barton made an ice cream slicer and an ice cream server in many of their patterns. The server in *Francis I* is illustrated here. The ice cream slicer is longer and allows the host or hostess to slice the ice cream, guide it onto the serving piece (illustrated), and finally place it onto the individual plate. A fish serving set can be put together using Reed and Barton's *Francis I* ice cream server and the vegetable serving fork in the same pattern (see Vegetable Serving Forks/Spoons, Figure 3.34).

Figure, 3.41, Ice Cream Knives and Servers (also known as Cake Servers): Stieff's *Corsage,* 10 1/8"; Gorham's *Strasbourg,* 10 1/2'; Whiting's *Louis XV,* 12 3/16"; Gorham's *Lancaster,* 9", and *Buttercup,* 10"; Towle's *Arlington,* 10 1/2"; and Reed and Barton's *Francis I,* server, 11 7/16."

The unusual and rare ice cream knife without a manufacturer's mark shown in Figure 3.42 is another outstanding example of the silversmith's art, especially the engraving. This knife appears to be made by Gorham in a series or flatware set labeled "Brick-A-Brack" (according to Samuel J. Hough in an article in May-June, 1989). The flatware consisted of six oyster forks, a slice and twelve ice cream spoons. The forks were made in the fall of 1880. None of the thirty-seven pieces in the set resembled the others. In the same article, Hough describes another ice cream slice, where the shape and the length were the same, but the engraving was quite different. One of the ice cream slices that was not shown with the set was labeled, "Number 150." In 1880 the cost for the slice was $20.50, gilting $1.25 extra, and a case for $3.25. Gorham records indicate that the engraving took seven hours. It would appear that this slice was made at about the same time.

Figure 3.42, Ice Cream Knife or Slice: Gorham, unknown pattern, 10 1/2".

The remarkable ice cream set in Gorham's *Cluny* pattern shown in Figure 3.43 is magnificent. This pattern first appeared in 1889, and represents a highlight in Victorian design. The designer was F. Antoine Heller. The beautiful design, while somewhat cluttered according to today's tastes, was executed with high quality hand workmanship. The bowls of the spoons are gold-washed with bright cut-work. The sterling bowl by Whiting adds a special attractiveness to this remarkable example of the silversmith's art.

Figure 3.43: An ice cream set in Gorham's *Cluny*, 10 11/16", four sterling ice cream spoons and an ice cream slice, with a Whiting Sterling repoussé bowl.

Waffle Knives & Hot Cake Lifters

The waffle knife is perfect for serving waffles and is handy as a flat server. It works very well to serve lasagna, casseroles and other oven-baked foods. Some knives have a small point on the front of a rounded blade, while others do not. The waffle knife in *Dauphin* by Durgin was identified by a page from an old Daniel Low and Company catalog of 1906. The waffle knife is usually all silver, and without piercing. The *Francis I* by Reed and Barton and *Lancaster* by Gorham examples are pierced, but they are exceptions to the rule. Most of the waffle knives manufactured by Reed and Barton have some piercing on them. In fact, the beautiful piercing of Reed and Barton's patterns is truly most distinctive and aids in identifying the work of Reed and Barton silversmiths.

The hotcake lifters by Kirk shown in Figure 3.44 are representative of hotcake lifters by this company. The *Repoussé* lifter and the *Mayflower* lifter resemble the tomato servers from this company, but the hotcake lifter is not pierced or scalloped. The *Mayflower* example has the characteristic cross-hatching design of old Kirk pieces. The Jenkins and Jenkins piece is unusual in the slight point at the top of the piece, and the small indentations at the point where the handle joins the blade.

Figure 3.44, Waffle Knives and Hotcake Lifters:
Top row: Durgin's *Dauphin,* 8"; Gorham's *Lancaster,* 8 3/16"; Reed and Barton's *Francis I,* 9 29/32"; Kirk's *Mayflower,* 8 3/4"; and Whiting's *Louis XV,* 8 5/16".
Bottom row: Kirk's *Repoussé,* 7 5/8"; and Jenkins and Jenkins, 7 1/8".

Wedding Cake Knives and Cake Saws

The wedding cake knife, distinguished by its hollow handle and long serrated blade, and the A.S. cake saw are very useful items. Most cake saws have small serrated edges on their cutting sides. At first glance the cake saw appears to be just another interesting collectible, but it is amazing how easily cake can be cut and served with the saw. Regardless of what type of cake is served, the saw does a beautiful job. The all-silver rarities, plain on one side and serrated on the other, are the best items to use with cake.

The saw side easily cuts the cake, and after cutting the knife can be reversed and the plain side inserted to lift up the cake. The wedding cake knife works well to cut and serve cake, but is perhaps even more useful for cutting and serving bread at a buffet table. French baguettes, wonderful with pasta, are easily served at the table with the guests cutting their slices and gauging the thickness of each slice to their own taste preference.

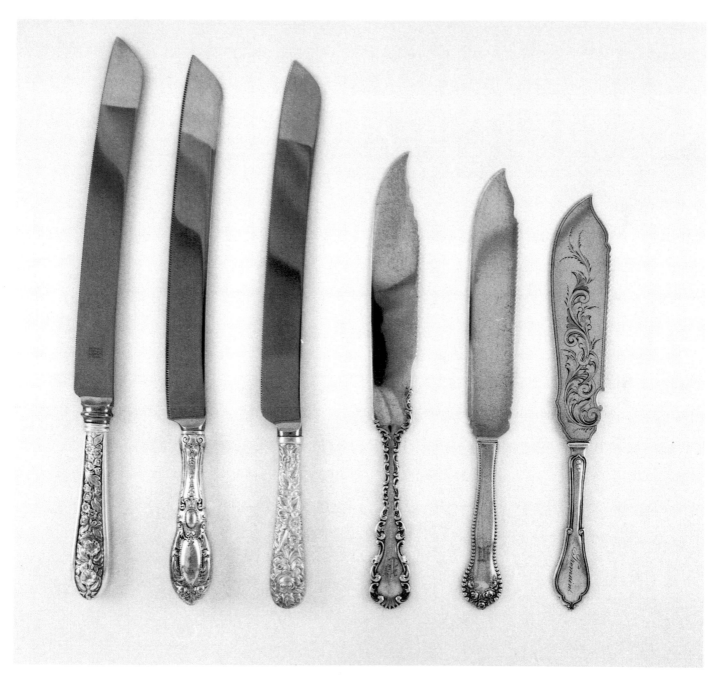

Figure 3.45, Wedding Cake Knives and Cake Saws: Stieff's *Corsage* wedding cake knife, 12 1/4"; Towle's *King Richard* wedding cake knife, 11 7/8"; and *Repoussé* wedding cake knife, 11 7/8"; Whiting's *Louis XV* cake saw, 10"; Gorham's *Lancaster* cake saw, 9 5/8"; and coin silver cake saw, 9 3/16".

Spoons

Berry Spoons

Originally designed to serve berries, these large bowl spoons are a necessity at large buffet dinners and are right at home for family dinners. Their size and shape make them useful for serving dishes such as curry and beef bourguignon. Most berry spoons have large bowls, into which some designs extend deeply. In Gorham's patterns *Chrysanthemum* and *Chantilly* (not illustrated) the manufacturer made not only a berry spoon but also a berry scoop, a large, unpierced, scooped serving implement.

The *Strasbourg* spoons are very useful because of the generous portions they can hold and the delicate design executed so beautifully in the silver. The large berry spoon in *Strasbourg*, when paired with the vegetable serving fork, makes a salad set large enough to serve a huge bowl of coleslaw or a green salad served in a small silver punch bowl for a large group.

The large spoon in Towle's *King Richard* has an unusually shaped, massive bowl. The lines and undulations swirl to create a most beautiful example. Towle's enormous spoon with a narcissus motif is a beautiful example of an Art Nouveau piece of silver. It is extremely heavy and represents a level of workmanship in silver and design that may never again be reached. Durgin's *Dauphin* example, with flowers extending into the bowls of the spoons, is typical of this company's workmanship. At the end of the top row the two examples in Gorham's *Lancaster* extend the shell motif beautifully into the bowls of the spoons.

The examples with fruit and flowers in the second row of Figure 3.46, as exemplified by the samples of Stieff's *Rose* with realistic strawberries and the small *Repoussé* spoon with flowers and fruit, lend themselves to serving fresh fruit salads. Stieff's berry spoons come in two sizes, and those with the berries were called 'Fruit Spoons'. Durgin's and Stieff's berry spoons came in two sizes, and those with the berry designs were also called 'Fruit Spoons'. Durgin's *Louis XV* and Gorham's *Lancaster* are typical of English berry spoons. There are few American-made berry spoons similar to these two examples, that is, with an oval shape and fruit and flowers in the bowls.

The oldest spoon shown, in a pattern called *La Rocaille* by Reed and Barton, is interesting from a design viewpoint: it is not symmetrical. Examples made by other manufacturers in the 1890s show a number of patterns with asymmetrical work, including *Luxembourg* by Gorham and *Louis XV*.

Tiffany and Company, the New York jewelers and silversmiths, made a large number of beautiful berry spoons with kidney-shaped bowls or elongated kidney-shaped bowls in some of their patterns. These spoons are highly collectible.

Figure 3.46, Berry Spoons:
Top row: Gorham's *Strasbourg*, 7 5/8" and 8 3/4"; Towle's *King Richard,* 9 11/16"; Towle's large spoon, no pattern name, 10 1/8"; Durgin's *Dauphin*, 9 1/8"; Gorham's *Lancaster,* 9 3/16" and 7 27/32".
Bottom row: Kirk's *Repoussé*, 7 1/2"; Durgin's *Louis XV,* 7 5/32"; Gorham's *Lancaster*, 8 3/4"; Reed and Barton's *La Rocaille*, 9"; Durgin's *New Art*, 8 13/16"; Stieff's *Rose*, 8 1/8"; Whiting's *Louis XV*, 8 9/16", and 7 1/2".

Bon Bon, Almond & Nut Spoons or Servers

Bon, bon, almond and nut spoons or scoops are small spoons with round bowls that are found in many patterns. The spoon's design helps determine its function. Some bon bons are scooped, some are pierced, and some are both scooped and pierced. Pierced spoons can be used to serve candied or seasoned nuts, as the piercing allows excess sugar or spices to fall back into the dish. Spoons that are not pierced can be used to serve parmesan or romano cheese at a pasta dinner. A collection of unpierced bon bon, almond and nut spoons could easily be used at a curry dinner to serve the various condiments.

Miss Manners, the etiquette expert whose column appears in newspapers and magazines, has called the bon bon spoon the most useless table utensil. Her reasoning was that the spoon did not fit the food (*Bon Appetit*, August 1993).

The top row of Figure 3.47 shows the wide variety that is available with these spoons. The two most unusual are the unknown central piece, due to its gold finish and fluting, and the *Louis XV* piece by Whiting, because it pours to the left. All of these samples are pierced with a variety of beautiful designs.

The middle row's large example in Towle's *King Richard* is regal because of its size. The unpierced examples in this row lend themselves to serving grated cheeses in addition to nuts and bon bons.

In the bottom row are three examples in Gorham's *Lancaster* which show the wide variety of scoops available in one pattern. Gorham did not make varied size pieces in all of its patterns. Most manufacturers made only one example. The Gorham unnamed floral piece is highly collectible because of the flowers and because it is not a named pattern. The smaller scoop in *Olympia* by Watson, Newell and Company is perfect for scooping salted or flavored almonds.

Figure 3.47, Bon Bon, Almond and Nut Spoons and Scoops:
Top row: Gorham's *Strasbourg*, 4 11/16"; Reed and Barton's *Burgundy*, 4 13/16"; Gorham's *King Edward*, 4 11/16"; *Buttercup*, 4 5/8"; *Twist*, unknown manufacturer, 4 9/16"; Towle's *Georgian*, 4 7/16"; Reed and Barton's *Marlborough*, 4 13/16"; Whiting's *Louis XV*, 5 5/8" and 4 17/32".

Middle row: International's *Prelude*, 4 11/16"; Wallace's *Grand Colonial*, 4 15/16"; International's *Theseum*, 4 11/16"; Stieff's *Betsy Patterson, Engraved*, 5 1/4"; Towle's *King Richard*, 5 7/8"; Stieff's *Corsage*, 5 3/8"; Kirk's *Primrose*, 5 3/16"; Durgin's *Dauphin*, 5 1/4"; and International's *Royal Danish*, 4 3/4".

Bottom row: Gorham's *Lancaster*, 6" and 4 3/8"; Kirk's *Repoussé*, 5 3/8"; Gorham's *Buttercup*, 4 19/32"; Gorham's floral pattern (no specific name), 4 7/16"; *Lancaster*, 4 11/16"; Watson, Newell & Company, *Olympia*, 4 7/16".

The various examples shown in Figure 3.48a, many of them by Schofield, illustrate the variety of usual pieces produced, from the nut shovel to the round bon bon spoon in *Baltimore Rose*, which can be used interchangeably.

Many patterns today offer only the bon bon spoon. In bygone years most manufacturers attempted to offer a greater variety of serving items for the silver-buying public. By always having something new to offer, their sales continued to show demand for certain patterns. Turner, in his book *American Silver Flatware* (1971), explains that Herbert Hoover, while serving as Secretary of Commerce, suggested in 1926 that silver manufacturers limit the number of sterling pieces available in any patterns introduced after that date. One of the primary reasons for Hoover's actions was to simplify the silver industry output. Customers had been able to order silver in regular, medium, and heavy weight sterling, causing a production nightmare for manufacturers and creating the need for retailers to maintain a tremendous variety of stock. This simplification might have made good business sense, but perhaps it should have applied only to place pieces. A large number of unusual serving and place items are available today to the serious collector because of the variety of items produced in available patterns made before 1926.

Figure 3.48a, Bon Bon, Almond and Nut Spoons and Scoops: Schofield's *Baltimore Rose,* nut shovel, 4 1/4", and bon bon, 4 1/16"; unknown manufacturer, unknown pattern, 4 11/16"; unknown manufacturer, unknown pattern, 4 11/16"; Schofield's *Baltimore Rose,* bon bon, 4 3/8" and 3 15/16".

Figure 3.48b: Resting beside a very rare three-section bon bon dish from Haviland are three variations of bon bon spoons in Gorham's *Lancaster* pattern; from top to bottom, a scoop server, a confection spoon, and a bon bon spoon.

Claret Spoons

Claret spoons are very unusual. Each has a small bowl-shaped or spoon-shaped receptacle at the end of a long, thin handle. Many of the handles are twisted and most have a decorative design on some part of the handle, usually on the opposite end from the bowl. Claret spoons were made in two sizes in some patterns, from the 1880s to about 1910. The original use of claret spoons is unclear but some dealers say they were used to pick up fruit from the bottom of tall cut-glass claret pitchers and to place the fruit into individual stemmed glasses. Others say the spoons were used to remove fruit from cut glass or china pitchers and to place the fruit on individual dishes of ice cream.

In Figure 3.49, note the two variations in the *Lancaster* pattern. One was made by Gorham, and the other is a variation sold by Shreve and Company. (See Made-Up Servers at the end of this section, Figures 3.89 and 3.90, for examples and additional discussion of these variations.) Whiting's examples' in *Louis XV* show the two variations in that pattern. The regular spoon shape of these two items may have been the forerunner of claret spoons, and later manufacturers made the newer versions with a ladle shape. Alvin's *Sorrento* spoon is definitely ladle-shaped, and it also has a pierced bowl. On the handle section, at the top of the long stem, the spoon is turned back. Perhaps this turning aided in holding the spoon, as the thumb would be used to apply pressure to the top portion. The name of these spoons brings to mind a question: why would these spoons have been created for claret, a red wine which was allowed to sit to let the sediment settle? It is also curious that these spoons have been developed and used with tall cut-glass or china claret pitchers, because using them together would have been quite awkward.

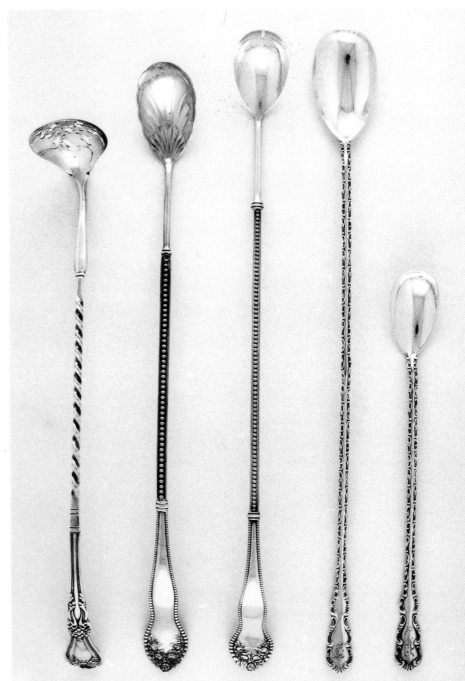

Figure 3.49, Claret Spoons: Alvin's *Sorrento*, 12 1/8"; Gorham's *Lancaster*, 13 5/8", and a Shreve variation of *Lancaster*, 14 1/8". The last two items are Whiting's Lemon Stirrers, Long-Handled (14 1/2") and Short-Handled (9").

Confection Spoons

Confection spoons are a slightly larger form of the bon bon spoon. They are larger in most patterns, and slightly different in shape (See Figure 3.48 b for photographs of bon bon, almond and nut spoons and scoops resting in a Haviland china piece that was designed to serve confections). In addition to serving confections, such as chocolates, these spoons can be used to sprinkle powdered sugar over gingerbread, cake or fresh berries. The handle rests flat, as does the bowl of this piece. In contrast, the pierced sugar sifter in Figure 3.70 is a ladle and its shape is better suited to different uses. Collectors can easily choose whichever silver item will work best with the food being served.

Figure 3.50, Confection Spoons: Gorham's *Strasbourg*, 5 5/16"; *Buttercup*, 5 11/32"; Schofield's *Baltimore Rose*, 5 13/16"; and Gorham's *Lancaster*, 5 7/8".

In Figure 3.51 the larger *Buttercup* piece is a confection spoon and the smaller item is the bon bon spoon. The size difference between the two is clearly shown.

Figure 3.51: Gorham's *Buttercup,* bon bon, 4 19/32", and confection spoon, 5 11/16".

Chocolate Muddlers

Chocolate muddlers are long handled spoons that are excellent for stirring up drinks and juices in crystal or silver pitchers. Originally they were used to stir hot chocolate in chocolate pots to prevent the chocolate from settling in the bottom. (Refer to the variety of individual chocolate spoons in Figure 1.46 and the two long-handled chocolate spoons in Figure 1.47 to put the three samples in Figure 3.52 into perspective.)

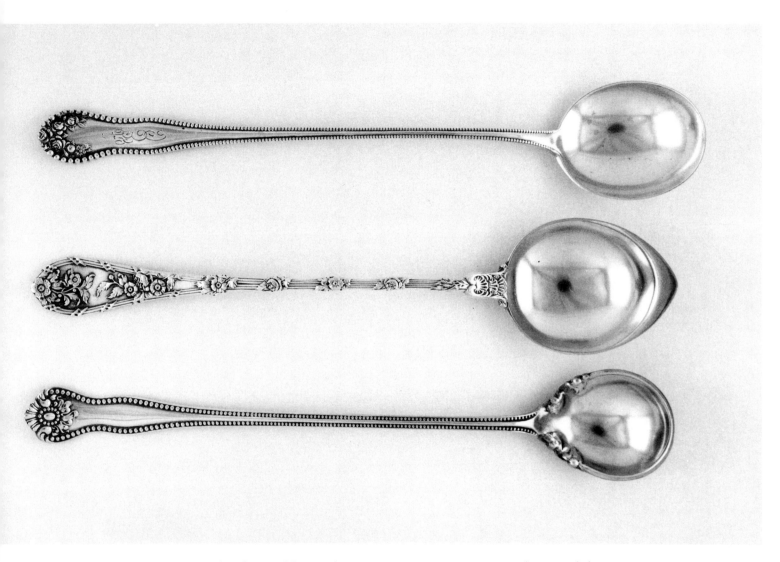

Figure 3.52, Chocolate Muddlers: Gorham's *Lancaster*, 8 1/4"; Durgin's *Dauphin*, 8"; and Alvin's *Wellington*, 8".

The accompanying picture, Figure 3.53, shows another use for the individual spoons. The individual spoons are being used to serve chocolate mousse in the Continental sterling holders with plated liners. A cream ladle in *Dauphin* is used to place whipped cream or whipped topping onto the mousse to be followed by a sprinkling of chocolate bits using the long handled chocolate spoon in the cut glass punch cup.

Figure 3.53: Another use for individual spoons—eating chocolate mousse from Continental sterling holders with silver-plated liners.

Horseradish Spoons

Horseradish Spoons have an elongated bowl that is about an inch long, placed at the end of a patterned handle that is approximately the length of a teaspoon's handle. The length may exceed that of a teaspoon in selected patterns, but shorter-handled spoons are the rule rather than the exception. The bowls may be plain, ribbed or have designs flowing into the bowl. Horseradish spoons are not used to serve a large portion because of the potency of prepared horseradish. After serving the horseradish onto their dinner plates, diners spread the horseradish with their own individual knife. These spoons were made in many patterns, but not in all patterns by all companies. Horseradish spoons can easily be adapted to serving other condiments and grated parmesan or romano cheese at a pasta dinner.

The Tiffany horseradish spoon was manufactured between 1891 and 1902. This can be learned by examination of the reverse of the spoon and finding the letter 'T' after the company name and before the mark "Patented 1895." Early Tiffany flatware, from 1869 to 1907, can be dated by looking at the letter following the firm's name. The following table (adapted from Kamerling, 1977) gives the letters that indicate when an item was made:

m = 1869-1875
M = 1875-1891 (the 'M' stands for Edward Moore, who headed the Tiffany silver department until his death in 1901)
T = 1891-1902 (The 'T' stands for Charles Lewis Tiffany, founder, who died in 1901)
C = 1902-1907 (the 'C' stands for Charles T. Cook, a former president of Tiffany's)

Comparing the bowls in Gorham's *Strasbourg* and in Towle's *Canterbury*, a difference is noted. The *Strasbourg* piece has a regular bowl shape, while the *Canterbury* spoon has a slightly bowl-shaped bowl. The *Canterbury* spoon would not carry much of the prepared horseradish to the individual's plate.

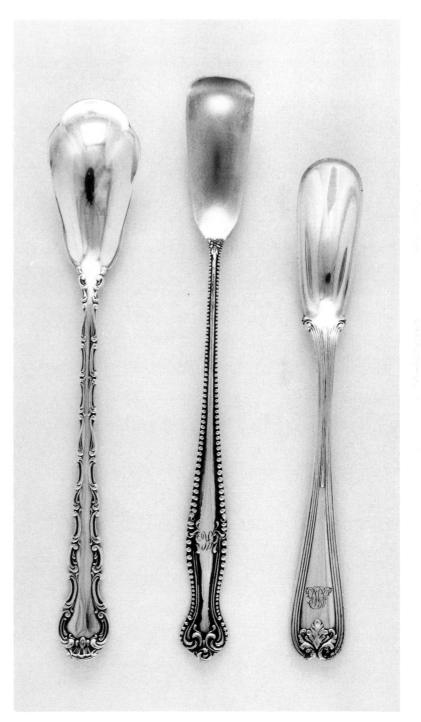

Figure 3.54, Horseradish Spoons: Gorham's *Strasbourg* 5 15/16"; Towle's *Canterbury*, 6 3/16"; and Tiffany's *Colonial*, 5 5/16".

Jam, Jelly, & Honey Spoons

Jam, jelly and honey have long been an important part of the first meal of the day and it is not surprising that silver manufacturers designed spoons for serving these toppings. All of the examples of jelly spoons shown in Figure number 3.55 have a slight ridge on one side to keep the jelly from sliding over the spoon's edge. Two sizes of jelly spoons are found in most patterns which can easily be seen in Figure 3.55. The largest three servers in *Repoussé*, *King Richard*, and *Grand Baroque* lend themselves, by their size, to serving small aspics and some cheese spreads as well as jam, jelly, or honey. In Durgin's *Fairfax* catalog, dated 1910 (when the pattern was introduced), the item currently being sold as a 'Jelly Server' was called a 'Honey Spoon', raising the question of why companies use so many names for similar items.

Figure 3.55, Jelly Spoons: Wallace's *Grand Colonial*, 6 1/4"; International's *Royal Danish*, 6 1/2"; Stieff's *Corsage*, 6 3/16"; Wallace's *Rosepoint*, 6 5/16"; Towle's *King Richard*, 6 7/8"; Wallace's *Grand Baroque*, 6 13/16"; Kirk's *Repoussé*, 6 11/16"; Gorham's *Crown Baroque*, 6 1/4"; *Strasbourg*, 6 1/8"; *Rose Marie*, 6 1/4"; and *King Edward*, 6 1/4".

The *Strasbourg* round bowl spoon is a jam spoon; however, a Gorham catalog from 1915 identifies this spoon in the *Chantilly* pattern as a Marmalade or Honey spoon. This is another case of a manufacturer changing the names and purposes for an item.

The *Lancaster* and *Louis XV* honey spoons are specialized serving pieces. The tip of the spoon bowl has an extra small point which was used to "cut" into the honey in a receptacle. Haviland china made an individual honey dish which was used at each place setting for dipping breads or meat into honey.

Figure 3.56, Jam and Honey Spoons: Gorham's *Strasbourg*, jam spoon, 5 6/16"; *Lancaster*, honey spoon, 5 15/16"; Whiting's *Louis XV*, honey spoon, 6 3/16".

Jelly & Preserve Spoons

Jelly was an important part of the Victorian table, and two sizes of spoons were available. The jelly spoon is usually smaller, and the preserve spoon is larger. Most manufacturers made both sizes in old patterns. The preserve spoon can easily be used for serving vegetables. The smaller of two Lenox vegetable dishes currently available provides the owners of jelly and preserve spoons with an excellent vehicle to showcase their collection (See Figure 3.57).

The two smaller spoons in Gorham's *Strasbourg* show the variations that can occur during the life of a silver pattern. Note the smaller spoon has much more decoration along the sides of the bowl.

Figure 3.57, Jelly and Preserve Spoons:
Top row: Dominick and Hoff's preserve spoon, *Renaissance*, 8 1/2".
Bottom row: Durgin's *Dauphin*, jelly spoon, 7 5/16"; *Strasbourg* preserve spoon, 9"; jelly spoon, 7 5/8"; (variation) 7 5/16"; *Lancaster*, preserve spoon, 7 9/16", and jelly spoon, 7 1/8".

Mustard Spoons

While many mustard spoons are shaped like ladles, they are nonetheless called spoons. The two spoons by Kirk on the right in Figure 3.58 are mustard or marmalade spoons. These are frequently mistaken for large master salt spoons by many dealers and collectors. Years ago, mustard was frequently made by mixing dry mustard with water and a touch of vinegar. When this type of mustard is made and used, it is important to rinse the silver spoon carefully or tarnish will appear quickly, and it is extremely difficult to remove.

Even though the *Strasbourg, Louis XV* coin silver examples and the *Lancaster* spoons in Figure 3.58a have ladle shapes, they are correctly identified as mustard spoons. The differences between the two *Strasbourg* examples is unusual. The smaller ladle is gold-washed for over half the length of its bowl and handle. This can be seen in Figure 3.58a; the darkening on the handle can be seen where the gold wash begins. Most frequently only the bowl is gold-washed, not the bowl and most of the handle.

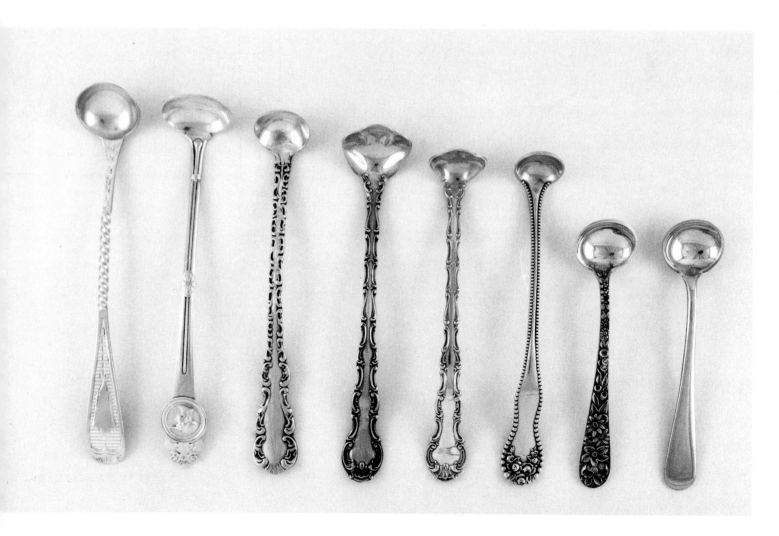

Figure 3.58a, Mustard Spoons: Marked Warner, unknown pattern, 5 1/4"; Gorham's *Medallion* (1864 patent date), 5 3/16"; Whiting's *Louis XV*, 5"; Gorham's *Strasbourg*, 5 3/4" and (variation) 4 5/8"; *Lancaster*, 4 5/8"; Kirk's *Repoussé*, 3 3/4"; and *Old Maryland*, 3 13/16".

Figure 3.58b: The same spoons used in Figure 3.58 here appear with a variety of mustard jars or pots, each of which calls for a different utensil. On the bottom are two additional spoons, one by Kirk in *Repoussé*, and one in Gorham's *Strasbourg*.

The mustard jars and pots include, at the top, an American cut glass container, at left a small cranberry piece, at right a clear glass container with a sterling top, and at the bottom a sample by Wedgwood in *Countryware* matching the china shown in Figures 2.38 and 2.39.

Nut Spoons

Nut spoons are used to serve shelled nut meats and are not frequently seen. Comparing nut spoons with other serving pieces would lead the collector to think that they were created from berry spoons and were heavily pierced. They would be very useful in place of pea spoons and slotted or pierced vegetable spoons. In some patterns the pea spoon is labeled as pea spoon/nut spoon, and some companies also refer to the ice spoon as an ice spoon/ nut spoon.

Durgin's *Dauphin* is typical of the Durgin work, with flowers and foliage flowing into the bowl. The delicate piercing is outstanding. Surely, some of the best piercing done on silver was performed in Durgin's Concord, New Hampshire silver manufacturing plant.

Figure 3.59, Nut Spoon: Durgin's *Dauphin*, 8 13/16". *Courtesy of Hank Thompson*

Olive Spoons

Olive spoons are quickly identified by a short or long handle and a pierced bowl. Most likely they were sold as a set. One of the examples in Figure 3.60a, the fifth item from the left, shows a long handled spoon with a small speared end. This particular item was probably used to spear olives. Any of these spoons can also be used to serve relish that contains a great deal of liquid, as the pierced bowl allows the liquid to drain off. The long pierced olive spoon with the pointed end traces its development from the sucket forks of the 18th century. Sucket was preserved fruit in sugar that was sometimes flavored with spirits. The fruit was speared, and served with a drink or to be eaten by the guest.

Figure 3.60a shows the long-handled spoons in Gorham's *Strasbourg*, in an unknown pattern, and in Whiting's *Colonial A, Engraved.* Most of these long-handled spoons were used with beautiful castors that held pickles or olives. The short-handled spoons, as typified by Gorham's *Strasbourg, Buttercup,* Durgin's *Dauphin,* Schofield's *Baltimore Rose,* Stieff's *Corsage,* and Towle's *Georgian,* show the variety to be found in the size of the bowls and the piercing.

These spoons are rather common and more easily found than some other silver serving implements. One silver company, Wallace and Sons, made a spoon called an "ideal olive spoon." The spoon usually had a long handle, and a bowl in which the entire center was removed leaving only a thin outer rim of silver. This assured the user of being able to remove an olive from the brine in which it was cured, and place it on a individual plate; the olive was held securely, unable to roll off the spoon.

Figure 3.60a, Olive Spoons: Gorham's *Strasbourg,* 5 5/8"; *Buttercup,* 5 11/16"; Durgin's *Dauphin,* 6 1/8"; Gorham's *Strasbourg,* 8 3/8"; unknown manufacturer, unknown pattern (marked "925/1000"), 8 1/4"; Whiting's *Colonial A Engraved,* 8 1/2"; Schofield's *Baltimore Rose,* 6 1/8"; Stieff's *Corsage,* 5 13/16"; Towle's *Georgian,* 6 3/8".

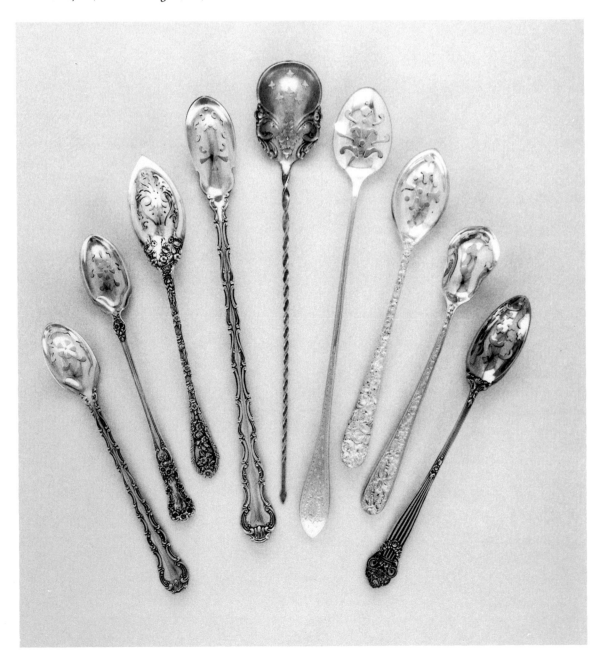

The relish dish in Coalport's *Indian Tree* shown in Figure 3.60b has three compartments in which to place relish. Each of the three sections contains a different kind of homemade relish and pierced olive spoons.

Figure 3.60b, Olive Spoons (right to left): Gorham's *Strasbourg*, 5 5/8", Durgin's *Dauphin*, 6 1/8", and Towle's *Georgian*, 6 3/8".

Pea Spoons

Old pea spoons are readily identified by their round, heavily pierced bowls. Most companies made pea spoons, but not in great numbers. Today Kirk-Stieff makes these spoons in a variety of patterns, including *Repoussé* and *Old Maryland Engraved* as pictured in Figure 3.61. Originally Kirk also made a large round bowl pierced spoon. The currently available pea spoon was originally the salad spoon and was not pierced. Today's spoon is pierced and vegetables can be left in their cooking liquid and served in covered vegetable dishes, allowing the vegetables to be kept warm longer. Some manufacturers labeled their pea spoon as a pea spoon/nut spoon, adding yet another detour for serious collectors. Other manufacturers labeled their spoon as a pea/ice spoon.

Figure 3.61 shows how the amount of piercing on the round bowl spoons varied from manufacturer to manufacturer. Shreve and Company's *Winchester* has the largest piercing, while Whiting's *Louis XV* is smaller. In this example the piercing radiates from the central portion of the bowl in a precision type design. Durgin's *Dauphin* is highly pierced overall. *Lancaster* by Gorham has a floral design in the center ringed with small, evenly spaced holes near the perimeter.

Figure 3.61, Pea Spoons: Kirk's *Repoussé,* 8 5/16"; *Old Maryland Engraved,* 8 5/16"; Shreve's *Winchester,* 8 1/2"; Whiting's *Louis XV,* 8 21/32"; Durgin's *Dauphin,* 8 1/2"; and Gorham's *Lancaster,* 8 21/32".

Salt Spoons

Salt spoons are fun to collect; collectors can build a large collection rather inexpensively and still enjoy the beauty of the various designs. Salt spoons come in two sizes. The large spoon is the master salt, and the small spoon is the individual salt. The individual salt spoon is the smallest spoon found in a place setting. (Refer to Figure 1.54 for a discussion and a picture of individual salt spoons.) Kirk's mustard spoon is frequently mistaken for the master salt (see Mustard Spoons, Figure 3.58). Smaller individual salts appear at each setting and may be shared with another member at the dinner table. The large size are easily used for a small individual serving of jam or jelly or with some oriental dishes. Additional uses include serving mustard or horseradish.

In Figure 3.62 the two spoons on each end, Whiting's *Louis XV* and Gorham's *Strasbourg*, each have a chevron shape. The other spoons, Durgin's *Fairfax*, an unidentified pattern from Simons and Brothers and Company, Whiting's *Lily*, and Gorham's *Lancaster* have round shaped spoons. It would appear that the round shape is more common in the design of master salt spoons.

Figure 3.62, Salt Spoons: Whiting's *Louis XV*, 3 9/16"; Durgin's *Fairfax*, 3 3/4"; Simons Brothers and Company, unknown pattern, 3 11/16"; Whiting's *Lily*, 3 7/16", Gorham's *Lancaster*, 3 9/16"; and *Strasbourg*, 3 5/8".

Stuffing, Platter, or Gravy Spoons

These very large spoons are frequently called stuffing, platter, or gravy spoons. At a festive table they are very useful for serving dressing from deep within the cavity of a large turkey. They are longer than tablespoons and have bowls that are slightly larger than tablespoon bowls. The *Lancaster* and the *Chrysanthemum* examples each has a "button back." The button was an old invention, placed on the reverse of the spoon to elevate it and aid in picking it up, perhaps because of the weight of the spoon. The *Strasbourg* piece does not have the button back. Through the years the *Repoussé* piece was made in several different lengths. The *Medallion*, at 12 $^{11}/_{16}$", is by far the longest spoon. It is in excellent condition and the cameo head design is still crisp and clear. The Whiting *Louis XV* spoon can be used as a stuffing spoon but it is part of the long handled salad set, shown in Figure 3.28.

Figure 3.63, Stuffing, Platter, and Gravy Spoons: Kirk's *Repoussé*, 10 3/4"; Gorham's *Lancaster* (button back), 12 3/8"; *Strasbourg* 12 3/8"; *Imperial Chrysanthemum* (button back),12 5/16"; *Medallion*, 12 11/16"; and Whiting's *Louis XV, 12*".

Sugar Spoons & Shells

One of the most commonly used serving items is the sugar spoon or the sugar shell. Some manufacturers made a plain spoon and others made spoons with a shell-shaped bowl, or even both kinds in the same pattern. In addition to changes with the bowl, many companies made two sizes of sugar spoons to better accommodate the varying sizes of sugar bowls. Many collectors purchase two examples of this spoon because of its highly adaptive nature. Other collectors carefully select sugar spoons for their collections to use for serving dessert toppings or parmesan cheese. In Figure 3.64 only Gorham's *King George*, Reed and Barton's *Intaglio*, Whiting's *Louis XV*, Towle's *King Richard* and Stieff's *Corsage* all have plain bowls. All of the other examples have either flower decorations or a shell design in the interior of the bowl. It is interesting that Gorham's *Lancaster* and *Crown Baroque*, even though they were introduced seventy-eight years apart, both have the same design in the bowl of the sugar spoon. The two colonial examples, Wallace's *Grand Colonial* and Reed and Barton's *Eighteenth Century*, both have a shell bowl design that harmonizes with the overall design. It is likely that the early sugar spoons with these bowl designs contributed the name "shell" to sugar shells.

Figure 3.64, Sugar Spoons and Shells: Durgin's *Dauphin*, 6 1/8"; International's *Frontenac*, 6 1/16"; Gorham's *Decor*, 6 1/8"; Wallace's *Grand Colonial*, 6 1/16"; Reed and Barton's *Eighteenth Century*, 6 3/16"; Gorham's *Crown Baroque*, 6 1/4"; *Lancaster*, 6 1/16"; *King George*, 5 7/8"; *King Edward*, 5 13/16"; Reed and Barton's *Intaglio*, 6 1/8"; Gorham's *Strasbourg*, 6"; Fessendon and Company, *Alice*, 5 7/8"; Whiting's *Louis XV*, 5 13/16"; Towle's *King Richard*, 5 13/16"; Stieff's *Corsage*, 6 1/16".

Tablespoons

The two examples by Stieff in the top row of Figure 3.65 show the delicate piercing of the first spoon, a large oval spoon, and the second spoon, used for the serving of rice. Alvin's *Orange Blossom* and Durgin's *Iris* are examples of two beautiful floral patterns. *Iris* was introduced in 1900 and *Orange Blossom* in 1905. *Orange Blossom* is currently being offered as part of the Masterpiece Collection by Gorham, the successor to the Alvin Company. The Tiffany spoon poses a question. The exact date is 1837 but Tiffany did not begin to manufacture their own sterling flatware patterns until 1869. This pattern is not in their pattern index, so Tiffany must have purchased it from some other manufacturers and placed their backstamp on the piece, a typical function of the time. The last two examples in Durgin's *Dauphin* show an original tablespoon and a pierced tablespoon, from the Masterpiece collection.

The first tablespoon in the second row of Figure 3.65 is Durgin's *Fairfax*, which was introduced in 1910. The pattern has been in continuous production as a regular part of the sterling line of Gorham, the successor to the Durgin company. Next is Gorham's *Strasbourg*, first introduced in 1897, and Wallace's *Grand Colonial*. These two tablespoons, one of which is pierced, are representative of the work that the designer, William Warren,

called "three dimensional sterling." The size of the bowls is different than most of the other spoons, and fits the overall design. The tablespoon in Gorham's *King Edward* is a standard spoon, but the last spoon is different. This spoon, in *Queen Anne-Williamsburg* is from the Stieff Company and is part of their Williamsburg reproductions. In this particular pattern, collectors can order regular tablespoons or ones like the example. The spoon is called "notched," and the reverse of the spoon is typical of silver made by early silversmiths. That is, the bowl appears to have been joined to the shaft of the spoon.

Most companies made a regular tablespoon and added pierced spoons later in the twentieth century. With pierced tablespoons vegetables can be served in their cooking liquid, which keeps the vegetables warm for a longer period of time. Companies such as Lunt offered a Buffet Spoon, which is really a tablespoon with a fancy bowl, for the same price as a tablespoon. Kirk also makes an oval shaped serving spoon in both large and small size. Tablespoons were made to serve food and were at one time an individual place piece, which accounts for some old sets with a dozen tablespoons. In European silver sets, all soup spoons are large and these are frequently mistaken for or used as tablespoons in our country.

Figure 3.65, Tablespoons:
Top row: Stieff's *Corsage*, 7 3/16", and (rice spoon), 8 1/8"; Alvin's *Old Orange Blossom*, 8 3/8"; Tiffany, no pattern name, dated 1837, 8 3/8"; Durgin's *Dauphin*, 8 1/4", and pierced, 8 5/16".
Bottom row: Durgin's *Fairfax*, 8 7/16"; Gorham's *Strasbourg*, 8 9/16"; Wallace's *Grand Colonial*, 8 1/2", and pierced, 8 1/2"; Gorham's *King Edward*, 8 3/8"; Stieff's *Queen Anne—Williamsburg*, 8 1/4".

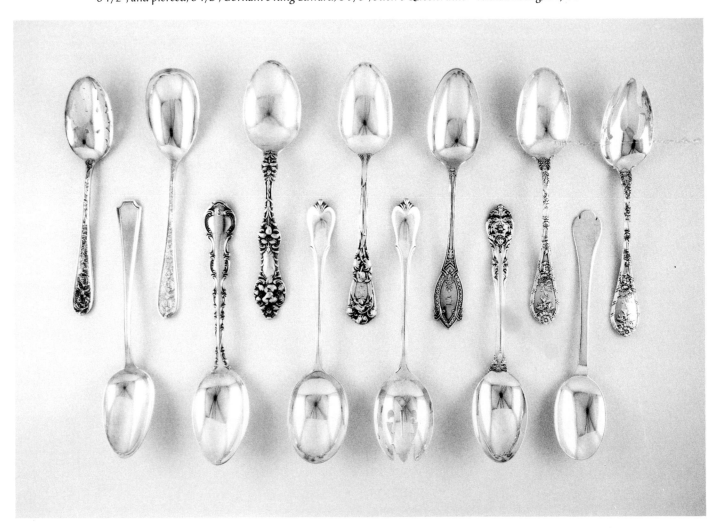

Vegetable Serving Spoons & other Large Serving Spoons

Vegetable serving spoons, sometimes known simply as serving spoons, are excellent for use at the buffet table. Gorham made a number of examples in many patterns, as did other companies. They also made an accompanying fork, which is larger than a cold meat fork and harmonizes in size and shape with the spoon in the *Lancaster* pattern. Kirk made two serving spoons with egg-shaped bowls in two sizes in some of their patterns. The medium spoon is 8 $^3/_8$" and the larger spoon is 9 $^3/_4$". The Stieff *Forget Me Not* is most likely this company's answer to the serving spoon. Whiting's example in *Louis XV* has a very large bowl and would make an excellent item for use at the buffet table.

Figure 3.66, Vegetable and Other Large Serving Spoons: Gorham's *Lancaster*, 8 1/2"; Stieff's *Forget Me Not*, 9"; Whiting's *Louis XV*, 9".

Ladles

Bouillon Ladles/Servers

Originally bouillon was a separate course, served into bouillon cups using a long, narrow-handled bouillon ladle. Most bouillon ladles have two pouring lips, one on each side of the bowl. At one time Gorham also made a bouillon server, with one large lip on the side of the bowl to serve bouillon at a formal dinner party. Today, either of these ladles can be used at small informal gatherings to serve punch from a covered vegetable dish or a small bowl. Bouillon ladles were made by most manufacturers and are readily available. They are often available at antique shows. Bouillon servers are more rare and are shorter but with a wider handle.

All of the bouillon ladles in Figure 3.67b are very similar. One reason for the similarity is that three are Gorham products, and the third is by Alvin, which became part of Gorham in 1928. The only difference is in the handle of the ladles. Gorham's *Lancaster* is twisted for a portion of the length of the handle. The other three either have a gadroon edge like the *Cambridge* piece, a floral handle like the *Poppy* example, or a grooved designed handle like the *Majestic* piece.

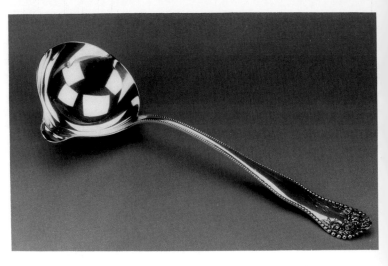

Figure 3.67a, Bouillon Server: Gorham's *Lancaster*, 9 5/8".

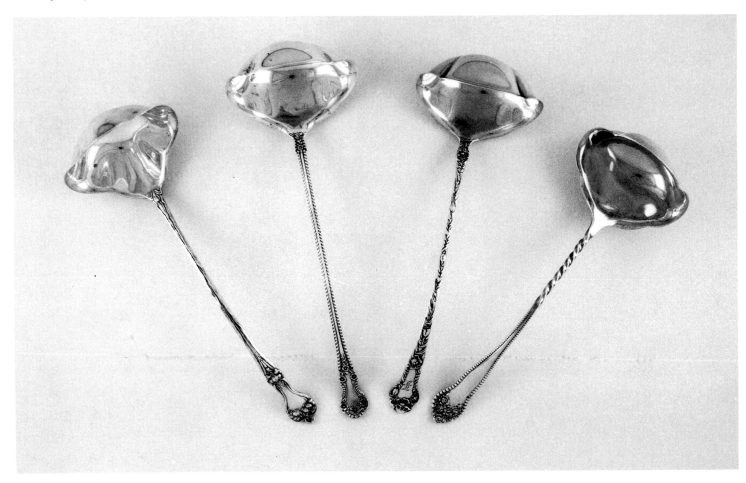

Figure 3.67b, Bouillon Ladles: Alvin's *Majestic*, 8 1/4"; Gorham's *Cambridge*, 8 3/8"; *Poppy*, 8 1/4"; *Lancaster*, 8".

Cream Ladles, Old Style & New Style

Cream ladles appear to be small versions of the gravy ladle and were originally used to serve thick cream at the table. Dominick and Haff's *Renaissance* in Figure 3.68 is an excellent example of a cream ladle. The next three ladles, all in Gorham's *Strasbourg*, represent the various cream ladles produced by Gorham. Cream ladles have undergone slight changes with the thickness of their handles. After the turn of the century Gorham introduced a new style with a wider handle, but the same size and shaped bowl. This was then called "new style." This is the first example in *Strasbourg*, on the left side of Figure 3.68. The current cream ladles by Gorham are rather thin-handled, as were the originals. For example, the second or middle *Strasbourg* ladle is in current production. The last ladle in this series was made by Gorham and is called a 'Cream Ladle, Small', which can be used to serve mayonnaise or a small serving of sour cream. It is a better ladle than the cream ladle for just a small serving. Two sets of these examples can be found in the top row in Gorham's *Strasbourg* and *Lancaster*. In *Lancaster* the ladles are in reverse. At the top of this row, and in the center is Towle's *King Richard*, with a fluted bowl. On the far right is Durgin's *Dauphin*, with a slightly larger bowl. The floral design in continued into the bowl as in many of the pieces in this pattern.

In the bottom row of Figure 3.68, beginning with Lunt's *Chippendale* with its delicate bowl, are a number of interesting ladles. Wallace's *Grand Colonial*, Gorham's *King Edward*, Wallace's *Rose Point*, Stieff's *Corsage*, and the wide-handled Gorham's *Crown Baroque* are very similar. Whiting's *Louis XV* with its fluted bowl is quite different. The last example in Reed and Barton's *Hepplewhite* is almost mid-way between the smallest and largest ladles. Reed and Barton also made two sizes in cream ladles, small and large, plus another ladle with a single pouring lip.

In a brochure promoting Gorham's *Virginiana*, the smallest ladle is called a mayonnaise ladle, which contradicts the examples within the Gorham line. This points out the fact that collectors who settle on a particular pattern should attempt to locate all the information about the pattern with a list of pieces or xerox copies of old sales brochures to make certain what it is they have found or have included in their collection.

Figure 3.68, Cream Ladles, Old Style and New Style:
Top row: Dominick and Haff, *Renaissance*, 5 1/8"; Gorham's *Strasbourg* in three variations, new style, 5 3/8", old style, 5 1/16", and small, 5 1/32"; Towle's *King Richard*, 5 15/16"; Gorham's *Lancaster* in three variations, small (or 'tete-á-tete') 5 3/8", Old Style, 5 1/8", and New Style, 5 5/8"; and Durgin's *Dauphin*, 5 9/16".
Bottom row: Lunt's *Chippendale*, 5 1/4"; Wallace's *Grand Colonial*, 5 9/16"; Gorham's *King Edward*, 5 5/8"; Wallace's *Rosepoint*, 5 11/16"; Stieff's *Corsage*, 5 3/4"; Gorham's *Crown Baroque*, 5 1/4"; Whiting's *Louis XV*, 5 9/16"; Reed and Barton's *Hepplewhite*, 5 7/16".

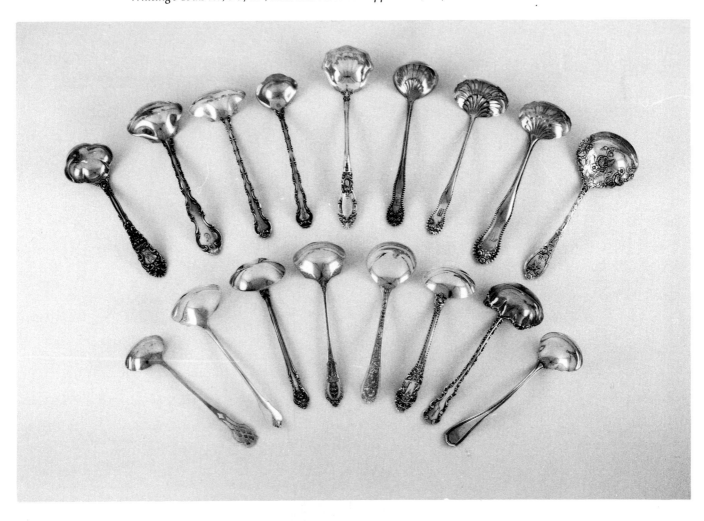

Gravy Ladles

Gravy ladles are a rounded or oval-shaped bowl at the end of a handle that has a graceful or bent shape. In figure 3.69 the many variations from a number of manufacturers and the wide range of shapes are easily seen. The shapes of the bowls in Figure 3.69 are all round, except for Gorham's *Strasbourg* and Towle's *King Richard*. These two patterns show a variation that is seen in most of the serving pieces in these two patterns. It seems that today many people have sidelined the gravy ladle to specific holidays as people only eat gravy on these special occasions. The rest of the year, ladles can be used to serve pasta sauces, or even salad dressing.

Figure 3.69, Gravy Ladles: Wallace's *Grand Colonial*, 6 1/8"; Reed and Barton's *Hepplewhite*, 6 9/16"; Gorham's *Strasbourg*, 7 3/8"; *Crown Baroque*, 7 1/4"; Durgin's *Dauphin*, 7 3/8"; Towle's *King Richard*, 7"; Gorham's *Lancaster*, 6 15/16"; *King Edward*, 6 3/8"; and Stieff's *Corsage*, 5 3/4".

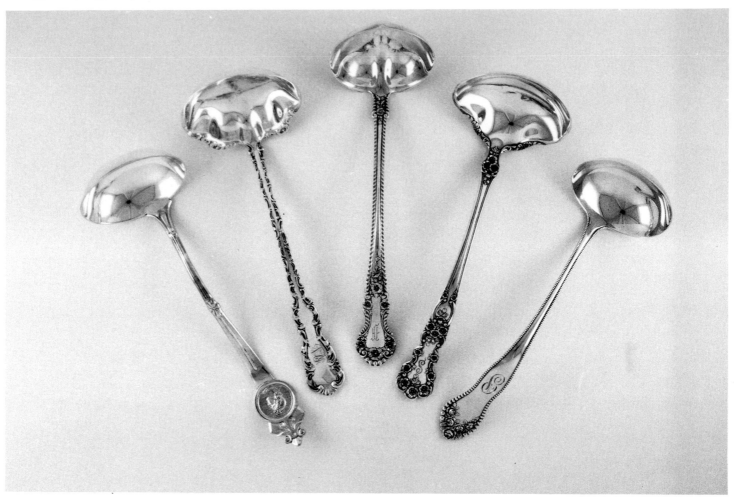

Figure 3.70a, Oyster Ladles: Gorham's *Medallion* (bearing an 1864 Tiffany date), 10 7/16"; Whiting's *Louis XV*, 10 1/2"; Gorham's *Cambridge*, 10 7/8"; *Buttercup*, 10 9/16"; and *Lancaster*, 10 1/2".

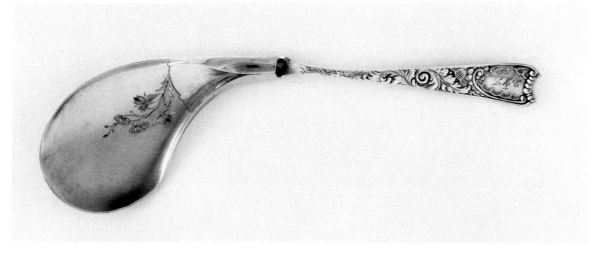

Figure 3.70b, Oyster Servers: Wood and Hughes' *Luxembourg* pattern. The shape of the blade and the manner in which it joins the handle is most unique. The silver blade overlaps before it joins the handle and has beautiful floral engraving. This piece and the other shown here exemplify the two types of implements designed for serving oysters.

Soup ladles are slightly larger than oyster ladles. Both oyster and soup ladles have a thicker stem than punch ladles. The bowls of oyster and soup ladles can be round or oval. They may have a pouring lip or two pouring lips and this may cause them to be confused with punch ladles. Oyster or soup ladles can double for punch ladles. Oysters were at one time served at formal dinners. The advent of refrigerated trains made it possible to send oysters many miles from the sea and they were transported across the United States into more and more American homes. Haviland and other china producers produced beautiful individual oyster plates for the eating of oysters. The Gorham *Medallion* piece, dated 1864, attests to the fact that Tiffany marked products sold by them with their own mark before they produced their own flatware. The crispness of the design detail is remarkable after more than a century of use. The examples in the Figure 3.71 show the variety of shapes in the bowls that were produced. The unusual pointed bowl in Gorham's *Cambridge* is unique. The oval bowl in *Strasbourg* carries out the same theme from other pieces in the line. The round bowls of the examples in *Lancaster* and *Louis XV* help call attention to the designs along the handles. Durgin's *Dauphin* again carries the floral design deep into the bowl of the ladle.

Figure 3.71, Soup Ladles: Gorham's *Lancaster*, 12 3/8"; *Cambridge*, 12 1/2"; Durgin's *Dauphin*, 12 3/4"; Gorham's *Strasbourg*, 12 1/2"; and Whiting's *Louis XV*, 12 1/2".

Pierced Ladles

Pierced ladles might be classified in the same category as cream ladles because some are wide-handled but others are not. At one time these items were called sugar sifters. The pierced ladle is the old style, as shown in Gorham's *Cambridge*, and the thin handle is the new style, as shown in *Lancaster*. Reed and Barton made pierced ladles in two sizes in *Chambord*, apparently using the gravy ladle for their large sugar sifter, and the cream ladle for their small sugar sifter. According to an old Gorham catalog this company did the same thing at one time. Basically the sugar sifter helped serve powdered or finely ground sugar onto berries and even pastries. Also pictured are examples in Gorham's *Lancaster* and *Chantilly* in the new style sugar sifter. The piece does not have a ladle shape and is very similar to the confection spoon. The example in Whiting's *Louis XV* is not ladle-shaped either. The outstanding *Medallion* piece in the center has a gold-washed, pierced bowl. The piercing had been meticulously done. This piece bears the mark of Wood and Hughes, and the stamp indicates it was manufactured after 1871, when they changed their backstamp.

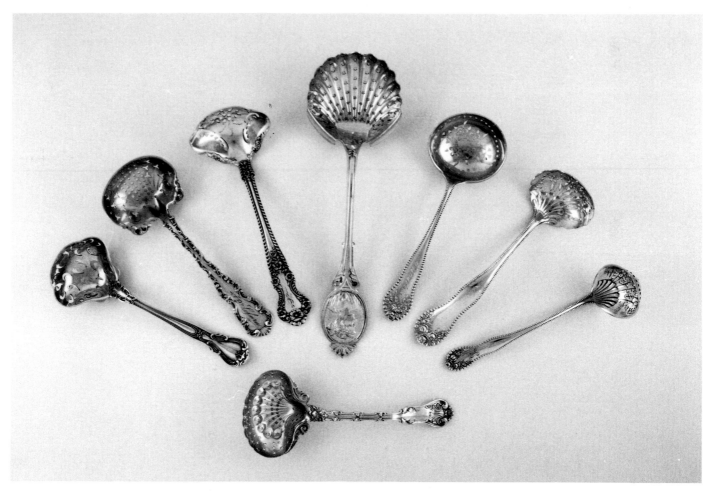

Figure 3.72, Pierced Ladles and Sifters: Gorham's *Chantilly*, flat style, 5 7/16"; Whiting's *Louis XV*, 5 1/2"; Gorham's *Cambridge*, 5 3/4"; Wood and Hughes, *Medallion*, 7 5/6"; Gorham's *Lancaster*, flat new style, 5 11/16", large size, 5 5/6", and small size, 5 1/4"; at the bottom of the figure, Whiting's *Imperial Queen*, 5 3/6".

Punch Ladles

A punch ladle can easily be identified by its thin, long handle, and its beautiful bowl that usually has two lips for pouring punch. The placement of the lips on either side of the bowl allows for either right- or left-handed serving. They were made in many old patterns and can usually be found at antique shows. The bowl of some ladles are gilded to protect the silver from interacting with the liquid, but others are not. Whether to use a punch ladle or one of the other ladles depends on the size of the bowl holding the punch. The punch bowl and the serving ladle should complement each other in size.

The example in *King Edward* by Gorham has an all-sterling bowl and stem placed into a sterling handle. Currently the bowl and stem are made in stainless and inserted into a sterling handle.

The third example, an early punch ladle made about the time of the Civil War, is part of a punch set consisting of a covered, enameled, cranberry glass punch bowl, tray, and individual cups. The design and shape of the ladle places it circa 1860-1880. This particular piece bears the mark of Vanderslice, a San Francisco jeweler and silversmith in business from circa 1858 to 1908. The pattern does not appear in pictured pattern lists for the Vanderslice Company. The original owner was supposedly one of the leaders in agriculture in the Central Valley of California, and this explains the grape motif. The two remaining examples, one in *Lancaster* by Gorham, and *Louis XV* are typical of the "true" punch ladle. Each is truly elegant.

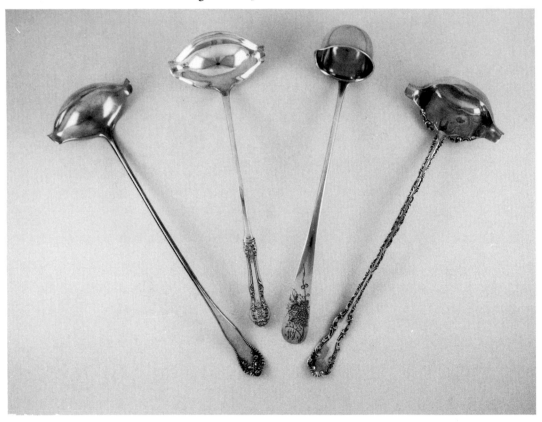

Figure 3.73, Punch Ladles: Gorham's *Lancaster,* 15 1/8"; *King Edward,* 13 1/8"; unnamed Vanderslice ladle, 14 3/8"; and Whiting's *Louis XV,* 14 15/16".

The second example, Figure 3.74, in Stieff's *Chrysanthemum* is for a right-handed person, as the ladle pours to the left. The bowl is gilded and quite large.

Figure 3.74 , Punch Ladle: Stieff's *Chrysanthemum,* 12 3/8".

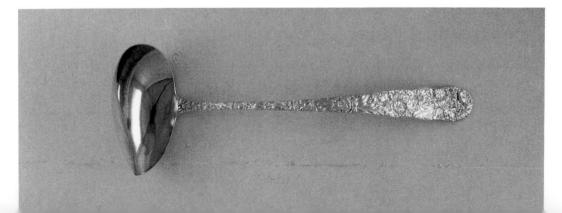

Tongs

Asparagus Tongs

Asparagus tongs are usually large implements used to pick up asparagus or sandwiches. These tongs originated with European silversmiths and were quickly copied by early American silversmiths. The tongs have undergone style and design changes, and the *Strasbourg* example, shown in Figure 3.75, is different from the original asparagus tongs which had a toothed part used to pick up the asparagus. This original asparagus tongs was replaced by the tongs in the illustration. Gorham made asparagus tongs in a number of patterns. Other manufacturers also made tongs, but asparagus forks are usually easier to locate. The tongs work well at a buffet table where guests can use them to quickly pick up and hold food they serve themselves. Occasionally, some manufacturers labeled these and similar large tongs as sandwich tongs. Again, readers are advised to locate an original catalog for exact identification. Tiffany and Company's asparagus tongs usually are found in a size similar to the Kirk tongs in the illustration. The Kirk tongs bear an old Kirk mark from the period 1846-1861. This pair of tongs have a flat side and a slightly curved side, and can easily double for sandwich tongs.

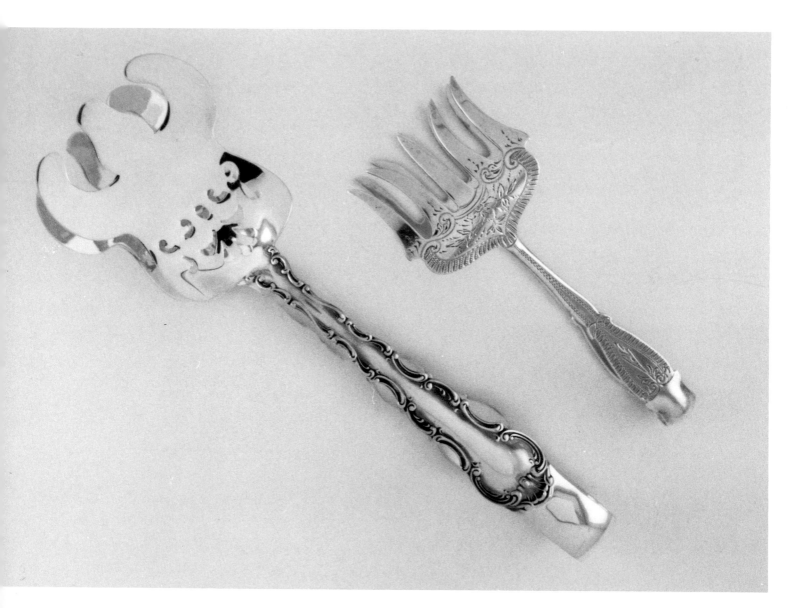

Figure 3.75, Asparagus Tongs: *Strasbourg,* 10"; and an unknown Kirk pattern, 6 1/8".

Ice Tongs & Ice Spoons

Ice tongs and ice spoons were designed and used before refrigeration was a regular part of life. At one time ice was delivered to each home and the chunks that were broken up were served with ice tongs or with ice spoons. Today the large ice tongs are very handy for use at a bar to serve ice or to place ice into goblets for use at the dining table. At a buffet table, a cache pot can be filled with ice and tongs can be used for guests to serve themselves the amount of ice they desire. Tongs can also be used to serve foods, especially hard boiled eggs or meatballs. Ice spoons, with their delicate piercing, can easily be used to serve vegetables cooked in their own juice. The examples shown in Figure 3.76 in *Lancaster, Louis XV, Strasbourg, Francis I,* and *Old Maryland, Engraved* have their own individual charm.

Ice spoons are found in older patterns. The example in *Louis XV* is magnificent. The piercing is very delicate, yet the gauge of the silver is such that it is very sturdy. The *Strasbourg* and *Lancaster* examples appear to be made from variations of the salad spoon, with the piercing added to the spoon.

Other examples seen from Tiffany and Company were very large round-bowled spoons, of tremendous gauged silver that were beautifully pierced. Again, the gauge of the metal was such that it could easily break up chunks of ice before serving.

Figure 3.76, Ice Tongs and Ice Spoons:
Top row, ice tongs: Whiting's *Louis XV,* 7 7/8".
Middle row, ice tongs: Kirk's *Old Maryland Engraved,* 6 7/16"; Gorham's *Strasbourg,* 6 5/16"; Reed and Barton's *Francis I,* 6 11/32"; and Gorham's *Lancaster,* 6 1/2".
Bottom row, ice spoons: Gorham's *Strasbourg,* 8 1/2"; Whiting's *Louis XV,* 7 7/8"; and Gorham's *Lancaster,* 8 5/16".

Sardine or Sandwich Tongs

Sardines were easily served with pair of beautiful tongs. In fact, tongs were probably easier to use than sardine forks because tongs grasped the slippery fish better. Sandwich tongs were made in some patterns, but not in all. To be sure which tongs a collector has it is necessary to examine a copy of the original design patent.

In the example of sardine tongs in *Louis XV*, note the curve in the last pair of tongs on the right. Both the upper and lower tongs have the same shape. The lower tongs were designed to be placed under the sardine, then the top would have been gently lowered, and the pressure applied so that the fish would not leave the tongs.

All the remainder of the tongs in this picture are sandwich tongs. The pair of sandwich tongs in Whiting's *Louis XV*, second from the right in Figure 3.77, has the bottom with a flat surface to place under a sandwich. All the remainder of the implements have a tined upper section and a flat lower piece. Gorham's have a tined upper section and a flat lower piece. Gorham's *Stasbourg* and *Lancaster* appear to be very similar, even to the piercing. Stieff's *Rose* has a top tonged section very similar to the tines on a pair of sugar tongs. The lower section of this piece is tastefully pierced.

Figure 3.77, Sardine and Sandwich Tongs: Stieff's *Rose*, 5 5/16"; Gorham's *Lancaster*, 5 11/16"; *Strasbourg*, 5 1/2"; and Whiting's *Louis XV* 5 3/16" (all sandwich forks); Whiting's sardine fork in *Louis XV*, 5 1/2".

Sugar Tongs

Tongs used for the serving of cube sugar have evolved along with the serving of coffee. They are usually found in two sizes, small and large. Both sizes are used for picking up cubed sugar. The smaller tongs were for use with demi sets, and the larger tongs for tea sets.

Figure 3.78 shows the wide variety of tongs that have been collected. The Kirk *Repoussé* is currently available. It is rather small, but perfect for demitasse. The two examples in Whiting's *Louis XV* are large, and the different claw ends may differentiate their purposes. The bottom row shows a variety of examples that invite comparisons. The first example, Towle's *Old English*, compares in size with the next pair of tongs. The next two samples, both in Gorham's *Lancaster*, illustrate the difference between large and small pairs of tongs. The next four examples, all in Whiting's *Louis XV*, allow comparisons from frontal and side views. It is possible to see how very closely the two sides are crafted. The last three examples, in Towle's *King Richard*, Gorham's *Buttercup*, and Alvin's *Prince Eugene*, show the variety of tine- or shell-shaped ends that could be placed at the end of the tongs.

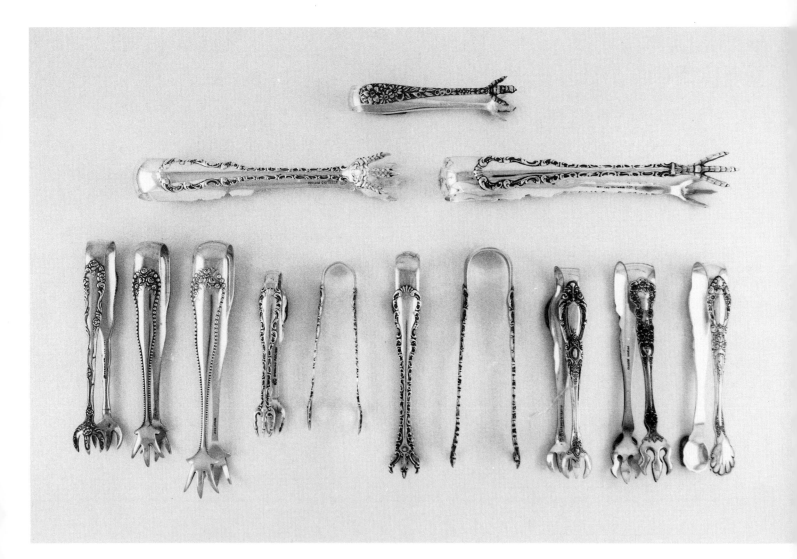

Figure 3.78, Sugar Tongs:
Top row: Kirk's *Repoussé*, 3 1/8".
Middle row: Whiting's *Louis XV*, 5" and 5 1/4".
Bottom row: Towle's *Old English*, 4"; Gorham's *Lancaster*, small, 4 1/4", and large, 5 1/8"; Whiting's *Louis XV*, small, 3 1/8", and large, 4 1/8"; Towle's *King Richard*, 3 15/16"; Gorham's *Buttercup*, 4 1/4"; and Alvin's *Prince Eugene*, 4".

Servers & Scoops
Banana or Pie Servers

Banana servers are typically long, sometimes pierced almost pie/cake-serving like items designed to serve bananas. The bananas can be baked, or just peeled, ready for a banana split. These particular items are found in only a few patterns and are difficult to locate. The example in *Lancaster* is very rare. The item was purchased as a banana server, yet a banana server cannot be located in any Gorham catalog. At one time a similar item, but heavily pierced, was seen in Towle's *Georgian*.

Figure 3.79, Banana or Pie Server: Gorham's *Lancaster*, 10 1/4".

Cake Breakers

A cake breaker is a highly specialized silver server with a sterling handle and a stainless insert that has many fine tines. Cake breakers were not made in all patterns. They are useful for cutting and serving angel food cake. The examples shown in *Lancaster, English Provincial, King Edward,* and *King Richard* are typical of this item. The *Lancaster* piece was "made-up." This serving piece was not available at the time the pattern was introduced.

Figure 3.80, Cake Breaker: Gorham's *King Edward*, 11 3/4"; Towle's *King Richard*, 10 1/4"; Gorham, *Lancaster* 10 1/2"; Reed and Barton's *English Provincial*, 11 1/2".

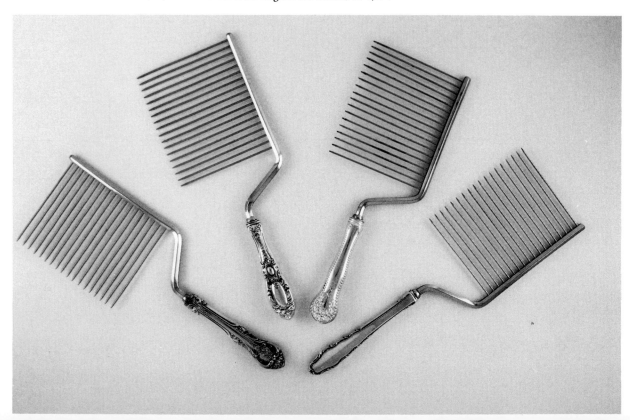

Cheese Scoops

Silver manufacturers made cheese scoops in two sizes, small and large. The *Buttercup* and *Lancaster* examples by Gorham in Figure 3.81 show the small and large sizes. The two samples in Whiting's *Louis XV* are also typical. The larger scoop has an almost closed top portion. These cheese scoops vary from those that are very open on the top to those that are almost closed. The *Francis I* example is typical of the smaller scoops, and the *Old Maryland* scoop is mid-sized. The larger scoops would be especially useful to serve portions from a whole cheese on the buffet table. Smaller scoops work well to serve soft cheeses like cottage cheese or ricotta cheese.

Figure 3.81, **Cheese Scoops:** Reed and Barton's *Francis I,* 5 13/16"; Kirk's *Old Maryland Engraved,* 7"; Whiting's *Louis XV,* 6 1/16" and 8 1/8"; Gorham's *Lancaster,* 8 1/4" and 5 7/8"; *Buttercup,* 7 11/16" and 5 15/16".

Cracker & Saratoga Chips Servers

Cracker and Saratoga chip servers are large scoops. Some are pierced and others are not. They are not found in all old patterns, but can readily be identified as to purpose by checking the bowl. If the bowl is pierced, it most likely is a Saratoga Chip (now called the Potato Chip) server (see the examples in *Lancaster* and *Louis XV*). If the bowl is not pierced the item is usually a cracker scoop (see the examples in *Lancaster* and *Louis XV*). Gorham in *Chantilly* and *Strasbourg* made a pierced server and called it a 'Cracker/ Saratoga Chips Server'. Every manufacturer had its own rules. An old undated brochure illustrating *Intaglio* by Reed and Barton shows the two servers, which appear identical, except that the Saratoga Chip Server has a small row of piercing at the bottom of the piece. None of Durgin's scoops that have been located have been pierced.

As the name suggests, this particular piece was made to serve chips that were served at the Saratoga spas in the 1880s. Silver manufacturers quickly made available to the public serving items for new food fads. Some of the fads were even for food that was brought to the United States during the period of the great immigration.

The Wallace *Rose* example is useful for serving small oyster crackers for the soup course. At a very large buffet, a large bowl, even of punch bowl size, could be used to hold a green salad to be served with a cracker scoop. A large china bowl used to serve pasta would also showcase a chips/cracker server.

Figure 3.82, Cracker or Saratoga Chips Servers:
Top row: Durgin's *Dauphin*, 8 5/8"; Gorham's *Strasbourg*, 8 3/4"; and Wallace's *Rose*, 8 1/42". and Whiting's *Louis XV*, 8 7/8".
Bottom row, cracker servers: Gorham's *Lancaster*, 7 13/16" and 8 11/16; Whiting's *Louis XV*, 8 1/4" and 8 7/8.

Croquette Server

The savory croquette, a specialty of fine French cooking, is usually cooked food held together by a thick sauce and deep fried. The example in Durgin's *Dauphin* is a perfect representative of croquette servers. The long handle with the beautiful piercing on the flat server side is masterfully done. This item is not frequently found.

Figure 3.83, Croquette Server: Durgin's *Dauphin*, 9 1/2". *Courtesy of Hank Thompson*

Macaroni, Entree, or Fried Oyster Servers

Among the more difficult items to find, macaroni servers, entree servers, and fried oyster servers can be mislabeled, and only the most knowledgable collector can identify them. Each manufacturer approached these serving pieces differently, and the result is a great deal of variation. Macaroni servers are usually comb-like (tined) in order to pick up the pasta. The *Francis I* piece has a small amount of piercing on the bottom of the piece, just enough to lift the pasta onto a waiting plate. The *Lancaster* pieces show both entree and fried oyster servers. The fried oyster server is the item with the fluted, somewhat bowl-shaped instrument. In *Chantilly* by Gorham, the difference is in the shape of the bowl and the angle of the tines. The macaroni server is slightly more bowl shaped than the entree server. The entree server is also more elongated in appearance. The smaller piece is the Macaroni server, and the larger piece is the entree server.

Again, the manufacturers have created a labeling problem, as some refer to the servers as macaroni spoons or macaroni knives or even as fried oyster servers. The label depends upon the manufacturer and the only way to know for sure is to check several silver catalogs from the same manufacturer.

Haviland designed a pasta bowl in some patterns. This points to the ability of the manufacturer to design what was needed as new immigrants began to move up the social ladder by introducing and making either silver or glassware or china to serve the food products typical of the culture. Today the pasta bowl is perfect for serving green spaghetti, made with fresh basil, parmesan cheese, pine nuts, and olive oil.

Figure 3.84, Macaroni, Entree, and Fried Oyster Servers: Gorham's *Chantilly*, macaroni, 8 7/16", and entree, 8 3/4"; Whiting's *Berry*, macaroni, 10 5/8"; Reed and Barton's *Francis I*, macaroni, 10 5/8"; Gorham's *Lancaster*, fried oyster, 9 1/2", and macaroni, 8 1/4".

Tomato & Cucumber Servers

One of the most versatile of all serving items is the tomato or flat server. There are many variations of this implement. The large, round, pierced server is perfect for tomatoes that are either fresh from the garden or warm from the broiler. Usually servers that are not pierced are hotcake servers (see the *Repoussé* server). The *Strasbourg* and *Old Maryland Engraved* pieces are all silver and pierced.

An old Gorham catalog shows a sliced tomato or cucumber server as one and the same, really clouding the issue. The 1910-1911 Gorham catalog which contains *Strasbourg* items shows the small toothed server as a small tomato server. The smaller round server in *Strasbourg* then becomes the cucumber server. Reed and Barton, in a brochure for *Chambord*, shows the large tomato server, and a smaller version with more piercing labeled 'Cu-cumber or Tomato Server, Small'. Between these two items, Reed and Barton shows an item labeled as a 'Fried Oyster Server', another example of how manufacturers changed their titles. Other manufacturers also made a small round server with teeth and called it a cheese server or a small tomato server, similar to the *Lancaster* and *Louis XV* small tomato servers.

Without an old brochure, collectors cannot be specific with a label. Some manufacturers, like Durgin, made the tomato server the same shape in both large and small and made the cucumber server different. The reader is also cautioned not to take any label as proof. There are always exceptions that can be found, since silver manufacturers took 'poetic license' in labeling their flat-ware or changed labels during the lifetime of a silver pattern.

Figure 3.85, Tomato and Cucumber Servers:
Top row, tomato servers: Gorham's *Strasbourg*, 7 1/2"; Towle's *King Richard*, 8 1/8"; Gorham's *King Edward*, 7 5/8"; Stieff's *Corsage*, 7 7/16"; Alvin's *Majestic*, 7 21/32"; Wallace's *Grand Colonial*, 7 3/4"; Gorham's *Lancaster*, 7 9/16"; and Kirk's *Old Maryland Engraved*, 7 3/4".
Middle row, various servers: Whiting's *Louis XV*, cheese or individual tomato server, 5 7/8"; Gorham's *Strasbourg*, cucumber server, 6 1/8"; Durgin's *Dauphin*, small tomato server, 6 3/4"; Gorham's *Lancaster*, small tomato server 6 3/8", and individual tomato server, 5 7/8".
Bottom row: Schofield's *Baltimore Rose*, small tomato server, cucumber or cheese server, 6 3/16".

Hollow-Handled Servers

New Hollow-Handled Servers

For many years silver manufacturers have used findings, inserts that were silver-plated or made of stainless steel. The findings were placed into the basic hollow handle used for knives, spreaders, carving implements, cake servers and the like. Currently most silver manufacturers have available a large number of servers, all of them sterling-handled, with stainless blades. The blades range from simple knife blades to salad serving forks, and salad serving spoons, large serving forks, fish serving knives, soup ladles, gravy ladles, stuffing spoon, lasagna servers, pasta servers, cheese planes, pierced serving spoons, rice serving spoons, shell serving spoons, and ice cream scoops. There are additional items such as butter spreaders and knives, pie and cake servers, and even cheese servers which should be included. The photograph shows a number of pieces manufactured in Wallace's *Grand Colonial*, and a Gorham lasagna server in *Dauphin*. The rapid introduction of these items may have been triggered by the rising silver prices and cost of producing an all silver item. The manufactured items are useful for serving a wide variety of foods, and allow the beginning collector to add a few serving pieces to a favorite pattern. Also the stainless steel finding can be considered an asset when serving foods that quickly react to sterling, as the stainless provides a barrier against almost all food reactions.

Figure 3.86, New Hollow-Handled Servers: Wallace's *Grand Colonial*, rice spoon, 9 11/16"; lasagna server, 10"; macaroni or spaghetti server, 10 11/16"; Durgin's *Dauphin*, lasagna server, 11 3/8"; Wallace's *Grand Colonial*, flat tomato or cranberry server, 8 13/16". At the bottom is Wallace's *Grand Colonial* ice cream scoop, 7 15/16".

Miscellaneous
Nutcrackers & Nut Picks

Nutcrackers were made in some patterns by the Gorham Company. The handles are sterling and the notched and toothed area which helps hold the nut for cracking appear to be made of steel. Some companies also made an individual nut pick, as shown in the *Louis XV* pattern by Whiting and the *Lancaster* pattern by Gorham.

Figure 3.87, Nutcrackers and Nut Picks: *Strasbourg*, nutcracker, 6 11/16"; *Lancaster*, nut pick, 4 5/8"; *Louis XV*, nut pick, 5 1/4". The nut bowl is silver-plated, from the Apollo Silver Company.

Bar Knives, Cap Lifters, & Bar Spoons

All the items made in this category use a sterling handle and a stainless or silver-plated finding. At first it appeared that all the items made in this category were from Stieff, but later the Towle examples emerged. These items, especially the hollow-handled items, could also be placed in the hollow-handled section, but because they are all related to the bar, they have earned their own category. The bar spoon in Stieff's *Rose* appears to be an iced tea spoon that is pierced. The bar knives in Towle's *King Richard* and Stieff's *Corsage* have a pick at the end for olives or onions, and a cap lifter section.

Figure 3.88, Bar Items
Left: Stieff's *Corsage*, opener, 5 1/2"; the center cap lifter is an all-over floral pattern—it may be *Repoussé*; Towle's *King Richard*, opener, 5 3/4".
Right (top to bottom): Stieff's *Rose*, bar spoon, 7 1/2"; Towle's *King Richard*, bar knife, 8 7/8"; Stieff's *Corsage*, bar knife, 8 1/4".

Tea Items: Caddy Spoons, Balls, Strainers, & Infusers

Tea was first introduced into England early in the 17th century. It rapidly became a part of everyone's diet and a daily ceremonious procedure. Throughout time a large number of items have been devised to help in this ceremony. At one time tea was kept in a locked container so that hired help could not help themselves to the expensive tea. When the locked container was open a tea caddy spoon was used to measure out the tea (see Figures 3.92 and 3.93). Tea caddy spoons were not made in all patterns, and they are not easily found. A strainer was also developed to help strain out the tea leaves from the liquid "tea," and these items were made in a large number of beautiful examples (see Figures 3.90 and 3.91). Tea balls (See bottom of Figure 3.90) held tea leaves as did tea infusers (See Figure 3.89), which were teaspoons with pierced, hinged lids to hold the tea. The individual tea infuser helped make tea perhaps more intimate.

Figures 3.89, Tea Ball Spoons (Infusers): Gorham's *Lancaster*, 5 1/2" (note: this piece appears to be made up, not original. A handle has been applied to a tea ball which appears to be silver-plate); Tiffany's *Wave Edge*, 5 15/16"; Paye and Baker, unknown pattern (made before 1920), 5 3/8".

Figure 3.90, Tea Strainers and Balls:
Top row: Gorham's *Lancaster*, 5 13/16" and 6 3/4"; Stieff's *Chrysanthemum*, 7 3/4"; Reed and Barton's *Francis I*, 7 1/16"; and Whiting's *Louis XV*, 6".
Bottom row: Unknown manufacturer and unknown pattern, 5 11/16"; unmarked tea ball, approximately 1 3/4".

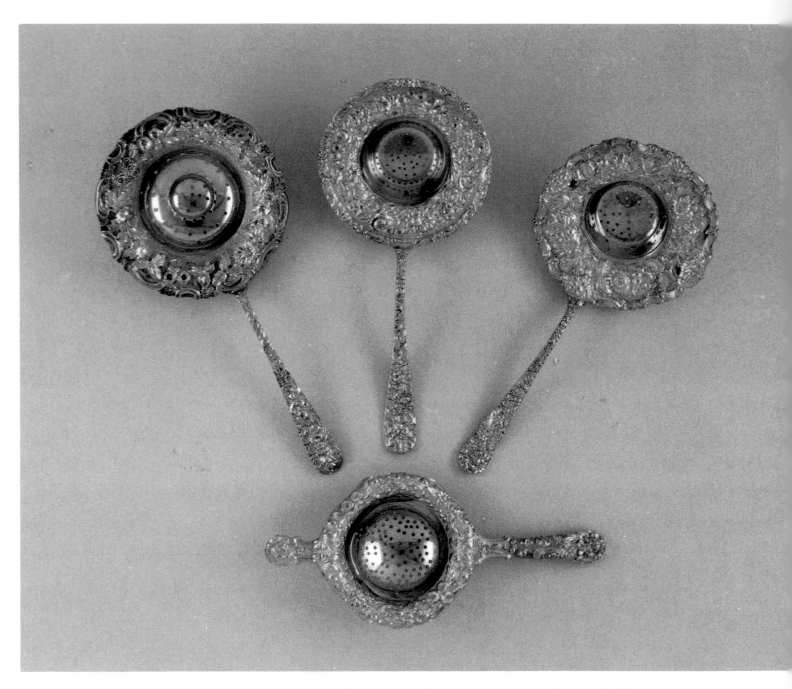

Figure 3.91, Tea Strainers: Jenkins and Jenkins, 7 5/8"; Stieff's *Rose*, 7 3/16"; *Chrysanthemum*, 7 1/8"; and at the bottom, Kirk's *Repoussé*, 6 5/8".

Figures 3.92, Tea Caddy Spoons:
Top: Whiting's *Louis XV*, 3 1/4".
Bottom: Durgin's *Dauphin*, 4 15/16".

Figure 3.93, Tea Caddy Spoons: Schofield's *Baltimore Rose*, 3 7/8"; Jenkins and Jenkins, 4 15/16"; and Schofield's *Baltimore Rose*, 3 3/4".

Made-Up Servers by Shreve & Vanderslice

Into this section a number of unusual items have been placed. They are here because they appear to be variants of serving pieces from either Gorham, Durgin, or Whiting. All of the items bear the marks of the manufacturer plus the jeweler's mark for either Shreve and Company or Vanderslice and Company. Both of there firms were started in the 1850s in San Francisco and at one time had extensive manufacturing shops. Each was in business until Vanderslice was sold to Shreve and Company in 1908. Shreve and Company is still in business at the corner of Powell and Post in San Francisco.

The items shown in Figures 3.94 and 3.95 appear to have been "made up" in the shops of Shreve and Vanderslice. Each of these firms must have had a licensing agreement with the silver companies or a lawsuit would most certainly have been begun by any of the aforementioned silver manufacturers. These made-up pieces are almost more beautifully designed than the originals. If the original manufacturer's pieces have been seen, these new examples stand out. The only "give away" to these items are their unusual ends, placed on sterling handles. How Shreve and Vanderslice did such quality work is remarkable. With the large number of examples found throughout the years, Shreve and Company and Vanderslice and Company must have made a large number of these examples and found that they sold very well. A distinguishing characteristic on some of the Shreve pieces is a dot at the base of the handle and added scrolls on the top of the bowl or the attached part. The reverse of the pieces, when carefully examined, barely reveal that these items have been attached. The pieces by Vanderslice are not so elaborately decorated, except for the large berry sppon with the scrolls and flowers seen in Figure 3.90. The figures show such a variety of examples that one can be sure that they must have made up an example for almost every serving piece made.

Figure 3.94, Made-Up Servers: Gorham's *Lancaster*, medium cold meat fork (Vanderslice), 7 5/16"; large berry spoon (Vanderslice), 9"; pastry server (Vanderslice), 9 5/16"; fish slice (Vanderslice), 10 3/4"; claret spoon (Shreve), 14 1/8'; large gravy ladle (Shreve), 8 3/4"; small berry spoon (Shreve), 7 11/16"; pastry server (Shreve), 8 1/4"; tomato server (Shreve), 7 13/16"; cold meat fork (Shreve), 6 3/4".

Figure 3.95, Shreve and Company: Whiting's *Louis XV*, beef fork, 6 11/16"; pie server, 9 1/8"; long-handled olive spoon, 9 1/4"; lettuce 9 1/2"; asparagus fork, 10"; large fish slice,   11 1/8"; berry spoon, 8 7/8"; berry spoon, 7 5/8"; and gravy ladle, 7 5/8".

Bibliography

Books

Agmew, Margaret Chason. *Entertaining with Southern Living.* Birmingham, Alabama: Oxmoor House, 1990.
Beeton, Isabella. *Mrs. Beeton's Book of Household Management.* London, England: Chancellor Press, 1986.
_____. *Mrs. Beeton's Household Management,* London, England: Ward, Lock and Company, no date.
Carpenter, Jr., Charles H. and Mary Grace Carpenter. *Tiffany Silver,* New York: Dodd, Mead & Company, 1978.
Chefetz, Shela, *Antiques for the Table,* New York: Viking Book Company, 1993.
Colonial Williamsburg Incorporated Approved Sterling Silver Reproductions, made exclusively by Stieff, Baltimore, Maryland, July 1940, Reprinted by Michael A. Merrill Inc., 1993.
Dolan, Maryanne. *1830's to 1990's, American Sterling Silver Flatware,* Florence, Alabama: Books Americana, Inc., 1993.
Giblin, James Cross. *From Hand to Mouth,* New York: Thomas Y Crowell, 1987.
Morse, Edgar W. (Editor), *Silver in the Golden State,* Oakland, California: The Oakland Museum History Department, 1986.
Osterberg, Richard F., and Betty Smith, *Silver Flatware Dictionary,* San Diego, California: A. S. Barnes & Co., Inc., 1981.
Practical Housekeeping , Minneapolis: Buckeye Publishing Company, 1881.
Rainwater, Dorothy, T. *Encyclopedia of American Silver Manaufacturers, Third Edition Revised,* West Chester, Pennsylvania: Schiffer Publishing Company, 1986.
Roberts, Patricia Easterbrook. *Table Settings,* New York: Bonanza Books, no date.
Sterling Flatware Pattern Index, 4th Revision, Radnor, Pennsylvania, 1989.
Stieff Handwrought Repoussè Sterling Silver, The Stieff Company, Baltimore, Maryland, 1920. Reprinted by Michael A. Merrill, Inc. 1991.
Turner, Noel D. *American Silver Flatware,* San Diego, California: A. S. Barnes & Company, 1973.
Woldman, Peri, and Charles Gold. *The Perfect Setting,* New York: Harry Abrams, Inc., 1985.

Articles

Cramer, Diana. "Eggs Eaten in Style," *Silver* 24 (January-February 1991): 21-24.
_____. "Claret Spoons and Jugs," *Silver* (March-April 1992): 35-37.
Hough, Samuel J. "Notes from the Archives: Brick-A-Brack Specialty Flatware," *Silver* (May-June 1989): 40-42.
Kamerling, Bruce. "Edward C. Moore: The Genius Behind Tiffany SIlver," *Silver* (November-December 1977): 8-13.
Soeffing, D. Albert. "Cuiller a Verre d'Eau," *Silver* (May-June, 1990): 21.

Catalogs

The "Buttercup," Gorham, Providence, Rhode Island, no date.
A Catalog of the Fairfax, William B. Durgin, Concord, New Hampshire, 1913.
Catalogue of the Sterling Silver Flatware by the Gorham Company, New York: 1910.
Chambord Pattern, Reed and Barton, Taunton, Massachusetts, no date.
The "Chantilly," Gorham, Providence, Rhode Island, July 30, 1895.
The "Chantilly," Gorham, Providence, Rhode Island, July 14, 1903.
The "Chantilly," Gorham, Providence, Rhode Island, July 27, 1903.
The "Chantilly," Gorham, Providence, Rhode Island, January 1, 1909.
The "Chantilly," Gorham, Providence, Rhode Island, August 1, 1910.
The "Chantilly," Gorham, Providence, Rhode Island, August 1, 1911.
The "Chantilly," Gorham, Providence, Rhode Island, May 1, 1912.
The "Chantilly," Gorham, Providence, Rhode Island, August 1, 1914.
The "Chantilly," Gorham, Providence, Rhode Island, February 20, 1915.
The "Chantilly," Gorham, Providence, Rhode Island, November 23, 1917.
The "Chantilly." Gorham, Providence, Rhode Island, March 26, 1928.
"Francis I" by Reed and Barton, Taunton, Massachusetts, No date.
The "Frontenac" by International Silver Co., Boston Massachusetts, no date.
Intaglio, Reed and Barton, Taunton, Massachusetts, no date.
The "Lancaster," Gorham, New York, 1898.
New Chantilly, Gorham Manufacturing Company, New York, 1904.
Price List of Tableware in Chantilly Pattern Sterling Silver, Gorham, Providence, Rhode Island, 1913.
Sterling Silverware By Kirk, Baltimore, Maryland, 1931.
Sterling Silverware by Kirk, Baltimore, Maryland, 1938. Reprinted by Michael E. Merrill, Baltimore, Maryland, 1992.
The "Strasbourg" by Gorham, Providence, Rhode Island. No date.
The "Violet" by Wallace, Wallingford, Connecticut, No date.
Virginiana, Gorham, Providence, Rhode Island, no date.

Charts—Place Pieces

These charts have proven very convenient for keeping records of sterling silver flatware. Collectors are encouraged to reproduce this page for use with their own collections. Each chart should be headed with the name of a particular type of item—Iced Tea Spoons, Asparagus Servers, Bird Sets, etcetera; the details of each piece in the collection can then be cataloged in a list below. The columns for insurance information provide a helpful reminder, but keep in mind that insurers require professional appraisals.

ITEM			Provenance			Date
Pattern	Cost	Monograms/Marks	Manufacturer	Insurance Schedule		Value
				Y	N	

ITEM			Provenance			Date
Pattern	Cost	Monograms/Marks	Manufacturer	Insurance Schedule		Value
				Y	N	

Charts—Serving Pieces

ITEM			Provenance			Date
Pattern	**Cost**	**Monograms/Marks**	**Manufacturer**	**Insurance Schedule**		**Value**
				Y	N	

ITEM			Provenance			Date
Pattern	**Cost**	**Monograms/Marks**	**Manufacturer**	**Insurance Schedule**		**Value**
				Y	N	

Price Guide

The market prices of silver flatware pieces fluctuate because of many factors, including the following:

—demand for a particular pattern
—geographical location
—rarity of the specific item
—condition of the item
—place of purchase (estate, dealer, etc.)
—just how much the purchaser wants the piece.

These prices for the items pictured in the book are given within a range, to take variations of this sort into account. This is only a guide, and these prices are not inviolate; items may be found at prices more or less expensive than these estimates. The reader is advised to know and learn as much as possible about items and prices. Some of the best ways to do this are to attend a number of antique shows and shops to look and talk to dealers, and to read widely. Neither the author nor the publisher assumes any responsibility for any losses that a collector may incur while using this guide.

FORKS

Dinner Forks	$45-95
Luncheon/Dessert Forks	$45-75
Place Forks	$45-75
Salad Forks, Large	$45-95
Salad Forks, Regular	$45-75
Salad Forks/Fish Forks, Small	$45-95
Fish Forks, Large	$55-95
Fish Forks, Small	$55-95
Dessert/Pastry Forks	$55-95
Pie Forks, Large	$55-95
Pie Forks, Small	$55-95
Pickle Forks/Knives	$55-90
Junior Forks	$35-65
Bird Forks/Knives	$65-95
Lettuce Forks, Individual	$75-125
Ice Cream Forks, Large	$45-125
Ice Cream Forks, Small	$45-100
Cocktail Forks	$35-75
Terrapin Forks	$65-125
Ramekin Forks	$45-100
Strawberry Forks	$30-65

KNIVES

Dinner Knives	$45-95
Place Knives	$45-70
Luncheon/Dessert Knives	$39-70
A.S. Luncheon/Dessert Knives	$65-145
Steak Knives	$45-75
Fish Knives, A.S. or stainless-bladed (A.S. knives are on the high end of the scale)	$65-145
Breakfast, Youth, or Tea Knives	$40-$65
Fruit Knives	$39-65
Butter Knives, H.H.	$30-60
Butter Spreaders, H.H. A.S.	$45-85
Butter Spreaders, Flat, A.S.	$35-85
Orange Knives, plated or A.S.	$65-125

SPOONS

Iced Tea Spoons	$39-75
Individual Muddler Spoons	$200-375
Dessert Spoons	$49-95
Place Spoons	$49-75
Large Round Bowl Soup Spoons	$55-125
Cream Soup Spoons	$49-95
Sorbet Spoons	$65-125
Parfait Spoons	$49-85
Ice Cream Spoons, Large	$49-95
Ice Cream Spoons, Small	$35-90
Teaspoons	$30-65
Pap Spoons	$95-145
Chocolate Spoons, Long-Handled	$45-125
Chocolate Spoons, Short-Handled	$45-125
Citrus Spoons	$45-95
Orange Spoons	$55-95
Five O'Clock Teaspoons	$30-59
Bouillon Spoons	$39-90
Egg Spoons	$75-145
Demitasse Spoons	$25-69
Salt Spoons	$10-30

CHILDREN'S SILVER

Infant Feeding Spoons	$40-65
Two-Piece Sets, Fork and Spoon	$40-95
Children's Silver and Youth Silver, Fig. 1.57	$50-95
Children's Knives, Fig. 1.58	$50-95
Children's Food Pushers, Fig. 1.59	$65-145
Food Pushers	$45-195
Youth Sets	$75-165

UNUSUAL PLACE PIECES

Lobster Crackers	$95-195
Individual Asparagus Tongs	$100-395
Individual Knife Sharpeners	$135-165
Individual Corn Items	$45-75

SERVING PIECES

Asparagus Forks	$195-650+
Asparagus Tongs	$195-475
Asparagus Servers, Hooded	$650-1695+
Bacon Forks	$95-195
Baked Potato/Sandwich Forks	$75-175
Beef Forks	$65-225
Butter Forks	$65-125
Butter Pick-Knives	$65-195
Butter Picks	$65-225
Cake Forks	$110-175
Carving Sets/Implements (Could be 2, 3, or more pieces)	$175-695
Cheese Forks	$195-245
Cold Meat Forks	$65-295
Fish Forks	$145-395
Fish Knives	$145-395
Fish Sets	$350-900
Lemon Forks	$40-98
Lemon Peelers	$75-195
Lettuce Forks	$79-145
Lettuce Spoons	$79-145
Lettuce Sets	$195-395
Pickle Forks	$65-295
Pickle Spoons	$65-295
Pickle Sets	$195-395
Piccalilli/Chow-Chow Forks	$75-195
Piccalilli/Chow-Chow Spoons	$75-195
Piccalilli Sets	$195-495
Relish Forks	$65-150
Relish Spoons	$75-175
Relish Sets	$175-325

Salad Forks, A.S.	$165-300
Salad Spoons, A.S.	$165-300
Salad Sets, A.S.	$165-595
Salad Sets, Wooden Tines/Bowls	$79-195
Salad Sets, A.S., Long-Handled	$550-995
Sardine Forks	$45-195
Sardine Helpers	$65-195
Sardine Sets	$145-395
Spinach Forks	$145-395
Toast Forks	$159-495
Vegetable Forks	$175-395
Vegetable Spoons	$175-395
Vegetable Sets	$250-795

SERVING KNIVES

Butter Knives, H.H.	$45-85
Butter Knives, Solid Silver	$45-165
Cake, Pie & Pastry Knives, H.H.	$65-95
Cake, Pie & Pastry Knives, A.S.	$129-495
Cheese Servers, H.H.	$65-95
Cheese Servers, A.S.	$65-295
Cheese Servers, Wire Cutters	$95-195
Crumb Knives	$295-495
Jelly Knives	$165-295
Ice Cream Knives/Server, A.S.	$125-495
Ice Cream Knives/Servers, H.H.	$65-125
Waffle Knife/Hotcake Lifters	$145-595
Wedding Cake Knives/Saws, H.H. Stainless	$65-145

SERVING SPOONS

Berry Spoons	$125-795
Bon Bon Spoons	$45-145
Bon Bon Scoops	$65-195

Claret Spoons	$195-595
Confection Spoons	$65-295
Chocolate Muddlers	$145-450
Horseradish Spoons	$85-395
Jelly Spoons	$45-195
Honey Spoons	$95-275
Jam Spoons	$75-195
Jelly/Preserve Spoons	$75-325
Mustard Spoons	$65-200
Nut Spoons	$195-495
Olive Spoons	$65-295
Pea Spoons	$175-650
Salt Spoons	$19-65
Stuffing/Platter, or Gravy Spoons	$165-595
Sugar Spoons	$45-135
Tablespoons	$45-195
Vegetable Serving Spoon	$175-295
Serving Spoons	$145-295
Fork and Spoon Serving Set	$395-795

LADLES

Bouillon Ladles	$195-495
Bouillon Servers	$295-595
Cream Ladles	$45-195
Gravy Ladles	$65-375
Oyster Ladles	$195-995
Soup Ladles	$195-995
Pierced Ladles	$65-325
Punch Ladles	$195-995

TONGS

Asparagus Tongs	$195-695+
Ice Tongs	$125-495
Ice Spoons	$165-595
Sandwich Tongs	$125-650

Sardine Tongs	$125-450
Sugar Tongs	$65-125

SERVERS

Banana/Pie Servers	$195-495
Cake Breakers	$75-165
Cheese Scoops	$85-450
Cracker/Saratoga Chip Servers	$295-595
Croquette Servers	$395-795
Macaroni Servers	$195-695
Entree Servers	$195-695
Fried Oyster Servers	$195-695
Tomato Servers	$79-495
Cucumber Servers	$75-450

NEW HOLLOW-HANDLED SERVERS

Various Items Shown	$45-125

MISCELLANEOUS

Nut Picks	$95-350
Nut Crackers	$195-550
Bar Knives	$45-125
Cap Lifters	$45-125
Bar Spoons	$65-145
Tea Ball Spoons	$125-495
Tea Strainers	$125-595
Tea Infusers	$145-495
Caddy Spoons	$75-450
Made-Up Servers	$65-750

The Indexes

Place Pieces

Serving Pieces

Pattern Names

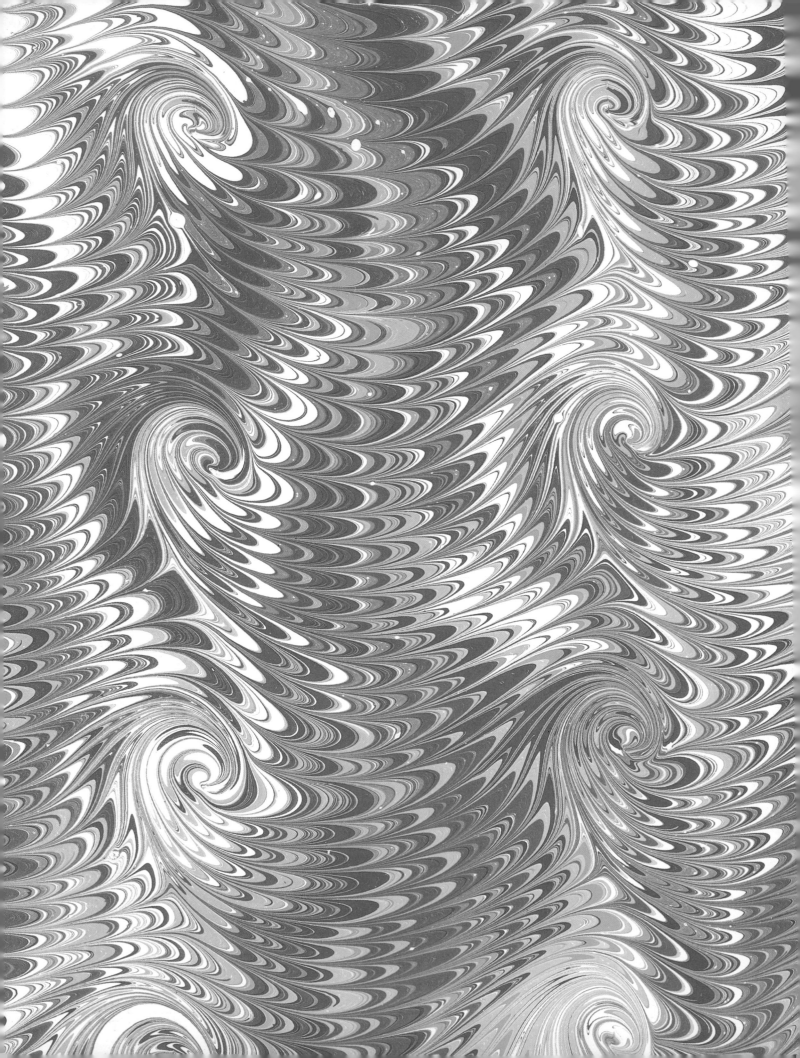